D0900016

SKYE

THE ISLAND & ITS LEGENDS

SKYE

THE ISLAND & ITS LEGENDS

By Otta F. Swire

With a Foreword by Sir William Tarn

SECOND EDITION

London · BLACKIE & SON LIMITED · Glasgow

Blackie & Son Limited
5 Fitzhardinge Street, London W1H 0DL
Bishopbriggs, Glasgow G64 2NZ

ISBN 0 216 89350 X

Printed in Great Britain by
Robert MacLehose & Co. Limited
The University Press, Glasgow

Foreword

GREAT numbers of people visit Skye every summer, attracted by the wonderful colouring of sea and mountain, and by the island's two unique possessions, the Cuchullin range and the Fairy Flag of Dunvegan; but about Skye, as Skye, so far as I know, no book exists. This book should fill the gap; but it does, I think, much more than that. For one characteristic of the island is that you will find quite a number of people who love it in a way shared, I think, by no other island of the West coast: people who understand, or are ready to understand, the meaning of the famous saying that Skye is not an island but an intoxication. That is a matter of *feeling*, which can no more be explained in cold print than any other form of love; but some of us know very well that it exists. It is the *spirit* of the island, of the land itself, and of the people who have made it; and I think this book goes as near to portraying it as one will get. The authoress has a great fund of knowledge of old legends and stories, customs and sayings, including various unpublished legends handed down by word of mouth; and one of the strengths of the book is the way in which she has caught and reproduced for her readers the *atmosphere* of a time long past.

Naturally the book has little mention of anything this side of the '45, and, like its material, deals chiefly with the Gaelic-Norse period; but this period itself rested upon an older stratum of forgotten peoples who often appear in legend as Sithe, 'fairies', and a few of whose place-names remain ; some of the creatures of legend, like blood-sucking witches, might go back to them. The Gaelic conquest was not complete; some septs, like the Macleods, were traditionally favoured by the older race and some even intermarried with them, while others made themselves hated; and some Sithe may really have been driven 'underground' and waged savage war against their dispossessors; the 'fairies' came largely to be regarded as evil. I can confirm by experience, though I cannot explain, the story in Chapter 5 of the great cliff in Trotternish called Baca Ruach; and I have heard of people feeling much the same about Ben Loyal in Sutherland.

But the bulk of the stories we possess, whatsoever their ultimate origin, belong to the Gaelic-Norse period, an age of heroism and savagery, tenderness and cruelty, loyalty to the death, and treachery and baneful superstitions; of people gradually groping their way towards the new light shining from Iona. It is therefore right that while the first chapter of this book relates the gruesome fate of some outlaws whose captain managed to raise the devil by roasting three cats alive, the book should conclude with the touching and beautiful story of the rescue from death of some little lost children by St. Bride and her oyster-catchers.

W. W. TARN

Preface to the Second Edition

In this second edition of *SKYE, The Island and its Legends*, a very few changes have been made to bring it up to date and also one or two Gaelic spellings have been corrected: otherwise it is unaltered.

I should like to thank the many readers who have written to me and whose letters were so encouraging and so interesting, and to apologise to those who suggested other spellings for Skye's great hills for not using any of them. I received seven letters querying or objecting to my spelling and giving the 'correct spelling'. Here are the seven 'correct spellings', with the authority quoted by the seven writers:—

Coolins,	authority	'Ordnance Map',
Coollins,	,,	'Ordnance Map',
Cuillins,	,,	Sir Walter Scott,
Cuilionns,	,,	'The name means Holly',
Cucullains,	,,	'Irish historians',
Chuchullains,	,,	'Well known ,
Cuphuillins	,,	'Because the name comes from a "P" language'.

Modern scholarship doubts the meaning 'Holly' and suggests that the name is probably very old and pre-Gaelic. As the Cuchullins have belonged to the Macleods of Dunvegan for nearly a thousand years, I asked Dame Flora Macleod of Macleod how she spells them. She replied that she used to spell them 'Cuchullins' (as I have done and as I know the 23rd Chief, Norman Magnus, did) but now usually spells them in the English form of 'Coolins', 'because it is straight-forward and easy for the English-speaking tourist world'.

I wish also to thank Mr. K. Macdonald of Applecross for most kindly helping me over Gaelic words.

OTTA F. SWIRE

ORBOST HOUSE
ISLE OF SKYE

June 1960

Acknowledgements

I WISH to express my thanks to Flora, Mrs. Macleod of Macleod, for all the help and encouragement she has given me, and for her permission to use the Dunvegan stories, especially the new 'Haardrada' theory of the Fairy Flag. I wish also to thank Mr. William Mackinnon, Glendale, and Miss Nicolson, Ord House, Sleat, for their help on the traditions of their districts.

Above all, I should like to thank my father and my husband for all they have done, for without them *Skye: The Island & its Legends* would have been neither written nor published, and without my husband it would have had no map.

O. F. SWIRE

ORBOST HOUSE
ISLE OF SKYE

Dedication

*To all the saints and sinners, heroes and Little
People, giants, water-horses, and other curious
creatures who look out from the past through
these pages, and to all the sons and daughters
of Skye, wheresoever they may have found a
habitation, I dedicate this book, for of their
deeds and thoughts is woven the spirit and the
treasure of the Isle of Mist.*

OTTA F. SWIRE

Orbost
Isle of Skye

Contents

CONTENTS

SOUTH SKYE

FROM THE GATEWAY
TO THE CAPITAL

A wise man once said:
'Skye is not a place but an intoxication'

1

Kyleakin to Broadford

———•◼•———

O come with me where the sea-birds fly
Remote and far by the Isle of Skye—
Away with the winds a-sailing!
Where dreams are the gifts availing—
Will ye come with me?
(From 'Come with me' by
Pittendrigh Macgillivray)

BORN on the site of Tyburn Cross and named after a pirate
ancestress who was hanged from her own yard-arm after
helping to raid Micklegarth (Constantinople), I feel that,
quite apart from my half-Skye blood, I should have much
in common with an island in which the King's writ has
never run—much—except by consent. 'For indeed', as a
Skye man remarked in 1749 on hearing that the long arm
of the law now reached as far as Ross-shire, 'it behoves
Christians to be very wary, for if the Lord Himself does not
check it, it will soon touch us here.'

Skye is a strange island in many ways. Those who visit it,
whether from choice or by birth, either hate it whole-
heartedly or else love it so dearly that they remain homesick for it until they die. And these latter are the great
majority. No one is ever indifferent to it, not even Government Inspectors! I am among those who love Skye and so
I want to write for my children some of the old Skye stories
which I heard from my mother and many of which she, in
turn, heard from a great-aunt who was born over 160
years ago, on 18 April 1799. That they may be of interest

to all, I have threaded these stories, as well as many which are better known, on the roads of Skye as on a necklace.

.   .   .   .   .

Kyleakin, the Skye terminus of the ferry from Kyle of Lochalsh on the mainland, lies in the 'giant' country where Fionn and his men once fought and hunted (see Chapter 17). These Fiennes were a race utterly unlike the giants of the fairy tales, and they exceeded men as much in virtues as in size. But the Fienne boys closely resembled their human counterparts and had a passion for stone-throwing, as witness Na Craigein.

It was a pet of a day when this Na Craigein (the Much Pawed) climbed Saigh Mhinn in the early dawn. Some say he was splayfooted, poor boy, but it seems more probable that his name only commemorates a certain puppy-like clumsiness. Be that as it may, the blue of sea and hill went to his head like wine and, desiring to play 3-pin ninepins against himself, he looked round for three suitable trees. As he looked he saw, several giant-miles away, an old woman carrying a milking-stool, a milk pitcher, and a cow-fetter, and approaching a cow in a very sly and furtive manner. Much interested, he lay down to watch and recognized the cow as one whose kindly old owner had often given him a bowl of its creamy milk, a rare treat to a Fienne boy accustomed to deer's milk. Seeing that the sly hag was about to milk her neighbour's cow, Na Craigein grew angry, picked up a large boulder and flung it to frighten her. Unfortunately he aimed too well and the boulder, Clach Chraigisgean, fell plumb on top of old woman, cow, milk pitcher, and all. Na Craigein was worried about the cow and started down to lift the rock off, but something else distracted his attention, so they are all still beneath the stone.

The many rocks and small skerries in the Kyles were also caused by Fiennes, this time grown giantesses (the Skye giantess Grein and a friend of hers in Raasay), throwing stones at each other during a quarrel, said to have arisen over the recipe for a face lotion made from deer's milk, honey, silver weed roots, and something else, but what? That was the question between them. Both were bad shots and the sea suffered.

Kyleakin (Haco's Strait) has been so called since Haco, King of Norway, anchored there with his fleet in the thirteenth century. At this period of Scottish history there was much trouble with the Norsemen who still held, howbeit loosely, parts of the Scottish mainland and the Isles. This trouble reached a head in 1263 when Haco came in person with the greatest fleet that ever left Norway, sailing past Lewis and down the Sound of Raasay to Kyleakin, where he anchored, and which has ever since borne his name. Here reinforcements joined him and he sailed on, his raven banners proudly flying, to meet his fate at the Battle of Largs.

After the battle he and other survivors took to the galleys but, as has happened more than once in British history, the weather now took a hand. Alexander III is said to have wisely avoided an encounter until a storm was seen approaching, so that after the battle the gale drove many of the undermanned fleet ashore. Ships were wrecked all round the coasts of Lorne and Mull and Skye. Haco himself with a few ships reached 'Wester Fjord' (Loch Bracadale) in safety. Here they came ashore, seized all the food they could find, and, leaving starvation behind them, sailed on to Kirkwall, where Haco, old, ill, and heartbroken, was landed to die. It is told that he had the old Viking sagas read to him and, contrasting their victories with his own defeat, died of grief and shame. Alexander III was afterwards known as 'The Tamer of the Ravens'.

To the east of the little town of Kyleakin a small promontory juts out, crowned by the ruins of Castle Maol. The main wall of the ruin, eleven feet thick, was cracked from top to bottom in the great storm of 1 February 1948, but Castle Maol still stands as 'saucy' today as when it was built in the twelfth century by 'Saucy Mary', a Norwegian princess, wife of a Macdonald of the time, who used the castle to extract toll from every ship which passed through the Kyles. It is said she had a chain across from the castle to the mainland shore. Some chain! Later, Castle Maol came into the possession of the Mackinnons of Strath.

The road from Kyleakin to Broadford is one of the best, from the motorist's point of view, in the island. It is also very beautiful but rather un-Skye-like, running, as it does in parts, through a birch wood. In the old days this part of Skye was densely wooded, covered by a part of the Caledonian Forest in fact, and so was the Island of Pabay which may be seen from the road. On Pabay are the ruins of a small chapel, traditionally one of those built by St. Columba's monks.

Pabay remained thickly wooded to the water's edge long after the forests had disappeared from the mainland of Skye. After the chapel fell into disuse and the monks left, it became a refuge of outlaws, 'broken men' and robbers, whose raids on the more law-abiding citizens caused much trouble. They are said to have met their end, as an organized raiding community, in a rather unusual manner. They had, of course, many enemies and their chief decided to rid himself of them all with the help of the Devil. So they made a great fire on the beach and roasted three cats alive with appropriate spells, an infallible way of raising the Evil One if you get the spells right. Several minor demons appeared, but the robber chief insisted that he would do business only with the Devil in person. At length Satan himself rose from the earth and asked their will. He was told to kill two men whom the chief feared. 'The price of two lives is two souls', said the Devil. This worried the band and an argument began. Now, the chief had been in the habit of boasting that if only he and his men could get swords that would not melt, they would conquer Hell and capture the Devil himself. Satan reminded him of this and offered to kill all his enemies and then return, with subordinate devils, and fight the band for their souls, 'here on the shore where swords do not melt'. This was agreed. Satan carried out his share of the bargain and returned. A fearful battle ensued, the Devil and his legions overcoming all the bandits who were armed with claymores or broadswords but failing to harm the chief, whose sword had a cross hilt. Suddenly a great black cat jumped from nowhere in particular on to his sword arm, causing him to drop his blade. He was never seen again. The blackened stones where the evil fire was lit and Satan stood may be seen on the beach near Ardnish in proof of the truth of this tale. But I have never seen them.

But to return to the forest that once grew where the road now runs. In it the 'little people' used to live. In Highland superstition there seem to be two quite different and distinct theories about the fairies—Celtic versus Scandinavian perhaps—which over the centuries have become confused. On the one hand they are represented as a people living side by side with their human neighbours and displaying most human characteristics. They wore the same clothes (though often of a bygone fashion), they had the same possessions such as cups, cows, distaffs, &c. But they had no iron and feared it. They borrowed and returned human possessions,

and sometimes stole them too. They showed great kindness
and gave much help to anyone who did a kindness to one of
themselves, but took revenge (often slyly) on anyone who
offended them. They were, in Skye, small and dark, and spoke
both Gaelic and a strange 'fairy' tongue. Flint arrow-heads
were 'fairy arrows'. In fact, they were the old inhabitants
of the land—the little dark Neolithic people, Iberians or
older, who were here before the Celts and who, as the fairies
or 'little people', show all the traits you would expect in the
conquered. They dwelt underground in the 'Picts' houses'
or 'fairy mounds', feared the iron they had never owned, and
took every chance to annoy those of their conquerors who
had not become their friends. It would be interesting to
know whether the belief that it is lucky to be 'first-footed'
at New Year by a dark man goes back to the time when
those who had made friends with the little dark people did
not lose beasts or gear.

The other theory makes the fairies or Daoine Sithe
some of the fallen angels. When the Devil and his angels
were driven out of Heaven some fell into the sea and became the Blue Men, whose chief stronghold was the Minch:

> *The Blue Men are breast high*
> *With foam-grey faces.*
>
> .   .   .   .   .
>
> *Then weary on the Blue Men,*
> *Their anger and their wiles:*
> *When billows toss*
> *Oh, who would cross*
> *The Blue Men's kyles?*

Some fell to earth and became the fairies. They hid from
God's sight in woods and caves and fairy mounds, wore
white or light garments, had supernatural powers, were

great musicians, and took the substance from all they wanted, leaving only the appearance, ready to crumble. Some remained in the sky and became the Merry Dancers, or Northern Lights, whose coming presaged storm or war or disaster. This last seems to owe something to the Scandinavian belief that the Northern Lights were the Valkyries, the 'Choosers of the Slain', riding to battle. In the early autumn of 1939 an unusually red and very brilliant display was seen over Skye and held by many to be a forecast of war.

The story is told that once, not very long after St. Columba's visit to Skye, a priest from Pabay was making his way through the forest to call on some of his parishioners. He came to a small clearing with a few scattered boulders in it and sat down to rest, sticking his crook in the ground beside him. As he sat resting, he became aware of sounds in the woods about him—faint rustlings and, as it were, voices—but all small and soft and definitely unhuman. He looked up and saw at the edge of the clearing a crowd of little people varying from three to four feet in height, but apart from that exactly like the people of his own time. Alarmed, he made the sign of the Cross, but instead of disappearing a little old man with a white beard, obviously someone of importance among them, came forward and, falling on his knees before the priest, begged his blessing for himself and his people.

'Who are you?' 'We are of the Daoine Sithe', said the old man, 'and we have come to beg you to pray for us, that we may become once more God's children and recover our souls. For a long time we have repented of our sins but we dare not say the Pater Noster or any other prayer unless we have received forgiveness.' 'Pray for you?' cried the scandalized priest, 'Give *you* my blessing? Never. For sins such as yours there is no forgiveness.' The old man groaned and was silent, but a little old woman stepped forward and dropped on her knees beside him. 'It is written "there is joy in Heaven over one sinner who repenteth", and that is true', she said, '"And him who cometh to me I will in no wise cast out", and that we believe', she pleaded. 'Pray for us.'

The priest was an honest man and her words disturbed him. But he remembered all he had been taught—the 'little people' belonged to the Evil One. They were evil. Had they not been driven out of Heaven? Such pity was but a temptation and he put it behind him and said firmly: 'There is no forgiveness for such as you. As soon would my stick become a tree again as God forgive you. Begone!' And he was alone.

He got up, much disturbed in mind, and, thinking of the faces of the little old man and the little old woman when he refused their plea, he forgot his crook as he went on his way through the forest. Everywhere round him he could hear as he went a soft, despairing wailing, as of a people without hope. It spread through the forest and up the slopes of Beinn na Caillich on into the hills and did nothing to lessen the trouble in his mind.

At last he reachd the hut he had come to visit, baptized a new-born baby, gave good counsel to its parents, not forgetting to add a warning to guard the child well as the 'little people' were about. When he was ready to leave, the child's father cut him a new stick from the forest, but the priest was anxious to find his old crook again, for it had been made for him by a fellow novice from a branch of the great ash near his old monastery on the mainland and was his only personal possession, so he carefully retraced his steps to the place where he had rested. He entered the clearing and, behold, there where his stick had been a magnificent ash tree stood, overtopping all the firs of the forest as God's mercy outreaches man's.

The priest fell on his knees and remained long in prayer. Then, sure of his duty, he arose and called the 'little people', but only the faint, hopeless wailing answered him. He went back to Pabay and sought leave to dwell in the forest, where he preached continually, day and night, the forgiveness of God to all who would listen, birds, beasts, and trees. Men called him mad and he never saw the 'little people' again, but slowly the wailing ceased in the hills.

Now to return to the road and to practical matters. About four miles from Kyleakin a road branches off to the left. This leads to Kylerhea Ferry and Glenelg (see Chapter 17). About a mile farther on another road takes off to the left, the road to Armadale and the south of Skye (see Chapter 18). From here onwards the road is lined with houses and crofts. First comes the township of Upper Breakish, then that of Harrapool, and then, on Broadford Bay, Broadford itself. It is now practically impossible for the uninitiated to decide where one township ends and another begins, so the three miles of 'ribbon development' is usually referred to in general terms as Broadford, but the hotel and cross-roads, eight miles from Kyleakin, where the Elgol road (see Chapter 19) goes left, is certainly Broadford proper. Corry and the hospital lie to the right, on the sea side, and the main road to Sligachan, Portree, and the north goes straight on. Beinn na Caillich looks down on them all.

2

Broadford to Sligachan

When death's dark stream I ferry o'er;
A time that surely shall come;
In heaven itself, I'll ask no more,
Than just a Highland welcome.

(Robert Burns)

BROADFORD itself, though not very big even for an island township, is a place of considerable importance in Skye and holds a unique position geographically, since all in Skye who wish to reach Kyleakin, Kylerhea, or Armadale, Skye's three ferry gateways, must pass through or near it, no matter whether they come from the north or the south. Equally, no one can go from the south to the north, or vice versa, except through Broadford.

Until World War II Broadford was itself a port, and one where the Portree steamer called morning and evening. Broadford Bay was always a joy to passengers, not only for the magnificent scenery—the mountains rising direct from sea-level are most striking—but also because a school of porpoises or a whale could almost always be counted upon to appear. Generally both were on view. I was once asked by a tourist what 'that' was, pointing to a spouting whale in the Bay. When I replied 'A whale' he grinned cheerfully and remarked, 'No use trying to pull my leg. Whales only live in the Bible and the Arctic.' But that was before the days of whale steak.

Unfortunately, in the war the Broadford pier fell into disrepair, a great loss to the township. Many representations to the appropriate Ministries eventually resulted in the promise of a grant in aid of one of two Skye piers, Broadford or Armadale. An embarrassing position, fraught with many snags for those who must decide on the relative needs, merits, and claims. But it became obvious that with her many buses and nearness to Kyleakin, Broadford had to lose. The other feature which adds to Broadford's importance in the island is her hospital, the largest in Skye.

Fairy music used often to be heard in Broadford, on the fairy knoll near the hotel. On the little promontory where Sutherland's garage now stands, fairies could be seen dancing. Whether they still do so, in and out the petrol pumps, is not known.

The road to Sligachan winds under the shadow of Beinn na Caillich, on whose summit a cairn can be seen. It marks the grave of a Norse princess who lies for ever gazing out to Norway, which she loved and whence she came. How was she ever laid there? What devotion she must have inspired in one at least in a foreign land. It was believed that if she saw danger approaching she would return to warn her children's children.

In about a mile and a half we pass a small bay or inlet, Sgianadan, where Dr. Johnson took boat to Raasay. From here there is a most excellent view of Scalpay, which island Dr. Johnson proposed to buy with the object of building a school and an Episcopal church on it. Probably this scheme was what caused Macleod of Macleod to offer Dr. Johnson one of the Colbost Islands as a gift, on condition that he dwelt there for three months of each year. The offer was not accepted! Boswell, however, reports the Doctor as being much intrigued at being addressed as 'Isay' and 'Isle Isay' while staying at Dunvegan.

Near here we pass through Dunan, noteworthy for its

beautiful red fuchsias, and then on to the township of Luib nestling under the hills. Luib two or three years ago was one of the most picturesque townships in Skye. Almost every house was thatched, and beautifully thatched—the work of craftsmen; situated on the sea-shore with the Red Hills as a background, it was well worth a visit to Skye to see it alone. But now, no doubt to the joy of the Health Authorities, these houses are almost all slated. Thatch is said nowadays to be dangerous; it holds germs. Probably this is true, but it also holds warmth and defies the draughts produced by a good south-westerly gale, no rare visitor, in a way slates do not. It was often renewed, and if serious disinfecting was necessary it could be, and was, removed and burnt. Now, if you want to change a modern slated roof after the children have had, say, scarlet fever, goodness only knows what permits and how many pennies would be needed. Besides, it 'isn't done.'. I think many people confuse a thatched house with a 'black house', a very different thing indeed. Black houses, however picturesque, are, I hope, a thing of the past. I can remember visiting one or two in my childhood but they were very rare even then.

The official sign of a black house was that it had a hole in the roof for the smoke to go out by, and no chimney. This made a great reek of peat smoke in the house itself, staining everything black, but also, it is said, disinfecting and killing germs in a way no modern house can compare with. All the same, even when you got used to it, it must have been very trying to live in. In my childhood such black houses as survived had generally had a chimney of some sort added to the hole. They usually belonged to old people, stained as brown as their walls with the peat smoke, who did not hold much with new ideas and claimed, probably correctly, that the fire did not draw nearly so well with a chimney. The making of a peat fire is a high art, whether on the floor or in a grate. It seems probable that the old belief, that if you did not 'smoor' the peat fire properly at night (that is, build it up and cover it with ashes to last till morning) the uncovered embers could and would open the door to the 'little people' or other evil things, arose from attempts on the part of the old to make the young and careless careful over this, since relighting, especially with damp peats, was not easy.

The floors of these houses were of trampled earth, flat and hard, and if you wished to empty a glass or a cup you just turned it upside down and the floor drank up the contents. The walls were papered with newspaper, picture papers, like a Christmas card screen, if they could be got; but as picture papers were very much rarer then than now, newsprint often had to do. I can still remember how fascinating those walls were. A built-in bed filled about half the room, and hens, as often as not, roosted under it. In the old croft at Biggeary, now a ruin, which I used to visit with my mother, the walls were papered with Queen Victoria's two Jubilees and the South African War. Its owner kept a pure Highland cow, a dear little brown beast, very tame, who used to come and welcome us like a dog and put down its head to be stroked, and I have never tasted such milk as she gave. A tumbler of it had only about an inch of milk at the bottom; all the rest was cream and it tasted of peat smoke, as also did most Skye eggs in those days. Curiously enough, when passing through Canada some years ago, we asked for milk for the children's supper, and the hotel at St. John provided just this same lovely cream which they called milk, but our small brats, brought up on what a Friesian cow calls milk, would not drink it.

The people who grew up in those old houses were extra-ordinarily strong and healthy: many not only live to a great age but, when they do, usually keep all their faculties. I know four of 93, 94, 96, and 98 years at present; only one needs glasses; three voted at the last election, and all can talk both in Gaelic and in English on any matter of the moment, though one, I admit, is a little deaf.

After Luib the road runs along the shores of Loch Ainort, a sea loch running into the midst of the Red Cuchullins who dabble their toes in its waters. It is hard to tell one hill from another when one is so close, for their foothills and shoulders run into each other in the most bewildering fashion. But, trying to follow the actual peaks, first after Beinn na Caillich comes Beinn na Cro, then Beinn Mhor; at the head of the loch stands Garbh Beinn to the south, with Marsco to the south-west and Beinn Dearg Mheadhonaich to the west, while on the opposite shore, which the road reaches in due course, is Beinn Dearg Mhor. At the head of Loch Ainort two mountain burns running down the lower slopes of Garbh Beinn to join into one small river make a most perfect and noticeable V of white foaming water against the dark hillside. This fact was never noticed until Winston Churchill made the V-sign, when it, in turn, became a sign and a promise.

Soon after the head of the loch is passed a road takes off to the left up through the hills. This is the old Druim na Cloich road, which was once the main road to the north. Druim na Cloich itself was a famous hill in the early days of motoring, with a gradient of 1 in 5, a sharp turn, and the surface of a mountain burn, which indeed it sometimes was. To have crossed Druim na Cloich in snow or ice was a thing to boast of. It soon became obvious that something must be done and two rival schemes were put forward. The one was a realignment of the existing road with, of course, re making; the other was the making of ten miles of new road, to be blasted out of the hillside and go, not over the pass, but along the slope above Loch Ainort and round the headland. Both schemes had ardent supporters, and as it happened that Macleod of Macleod took one view and the Macdonald Estate the other, feeling ran high, almost as high as in the old days of clan feuds! In the end the County Council adopted the new road scheme and, amid dire prophecies of all winter users being blown into the sea, it went forward.

These prophecies were not fulfilled but the road did prove dangerous in winter, so a new one which follows the old Druim na Cloich road in part has recently been opened. It leaves the 'old new road' near the head of Loch Ainort and rejoins it just before Sconser. A wonderful drive through the great hills while Glamaig looks down. At her foot stands Sconser Lodge, now a hotel but once the Lodge of the Macdonald deer forest where the legendary Fiennes used to hunt and kill five or six thousand deer in a day.

It was at Sconser Inn that Clanranald, emissary of Prince Charles Edward, met the Chiefs of Macdonald and Macleod when he came to beg for their assistance on the Prince's behalf in 1745. But he was too late. President Forbes had got his views in first, which may well have been a blessing for the island. Both Macleod and Macdonald summoned their clans to fight, not for Prince Charles but for King George. Both got a poor response (as they probably anticipated) for on the whole Skye's sympathies were Jacobite. Many private individuals in the island followed Clanranald to the Prince.

Sconser Inn, was honoured too, by a visit from Dr. Johnson.

Both Loch Sligachan and Loch Ainort are great haunts of wild birds; wild geese and many varieties of duck can be seen there in the winter. At the head of Loch Sligachan is the well-known Sligachan Hotel, favourite base for mountaineers and artists.

3

The Cuchullins

For rarely human eye has known
A scene so stern . . .

  . . . . .

Coriskin call the dark lake's name,
Coolin the ridge, as bards proclaim,
From old Cuchullin, chief of fame.

  . . . .

Or that your eye could see the mood
Of Corryvrekin's whirlpool rude,
When dons the Hag her whiten'd hood.

(From *The Lord of the Isles*
by Sir Walter Scott)

MANY books and articles on the Cuchullins have been written from the point of view of the mountaineer, and innumerable artists have painted innumerable pictures of them. No words and few pictures can do justice to their beauty, and their peculiar charm is not to be captured by pen or brush. But no one who has seen them, black against the clear green and yellow of a summer sunrise or tinted soft rose pink by an autumn sunset, can ever forget.

In any case, I have no intention of vying with the climbers who write of them. This chapter will be simply from the point of view of an earthworm with his, perhaps limited, outlook.

If you consider the Cuchullins and the Red Hills, the most striking thing is the difference between them. The

Red Hills, or Red Cuchullins (both names much used), are round-topped, shale-covered mountains and their deep red colouring is often most noticeable. The Black Cuchullins are as dark as their name, a mass of pinnacles and sharp rock ridges violently indented against the sky. The fruit of some fierce world upheaval, they are yet friendly hills. They are 'black' almost all the year, for although there are many peaks of 3,000 feet and over, snow rarely lies on them, and when they are snow-clad it seldom lasts. Lower hills such as Storr (2,360 feet) may be snow-white for days on end and the Red Hills snow-topped, when the Cuchullins hold only a sprinkling for a matter of hours. The reason is this:

When all the world was new, there was a great heather-clad plain between Loch Bracadale on the west and the Red Hills on the east. It was a dark and lonely place and the Cailleach Bhur (= Hag of the Ridges, i.e. Winter), whose home was on Ben Wyvis, often lived there when she came west to boil up her linen in her washing pot, danger-ous Corryvreckan. She was a very powerful and fearsome person who had made Scotland by dropping into the sea a creel of peat and rock which she brought with her from the north. When her clothes had boiled well, she would spread them to bleach on Storr, and while she was in Skye no good weather was to be got at all. Now Spring hated her because she held the maiden he loved prisoner (until the girl should wash a brown fleece white) and he fought with her, but she was strong, stronger than anyone else within the four brown boundaries of the earth, and he could do nothing. He appealed to the Sun to help him and the Sun flung his spear at Cailleach Bhur as she walked on the moor; it was so fiery and hot it scorched the very earth, and where it struck, a blister, six miles long and six miles

Loch Poultiel and Dunvegan Head from Glendale

Camasunary Bay. Loch Scavaig extreme left, Marsco right centre

wide, grew and grew until it burst and flung forth the Cuchullins as a glowing, molten mass. For many, many months they glowed and smoked, and the Cailleach Bhur fled away and hid beneath the roots of a holly and dared not return. Even now, her snow is useless against the fire hills.

For a long time no living thing inhabited the Cuchullins, and then came Skiach—goddess or mortal no one knows which, but undoubtedly a great warrior. She started a school for heroes in the mountains, to teach them the art of war. Some say she took her name from a Gaelic name for Skye, others that Skye took its name from her. However that may be, the fame of the name and of her school spread abroad and reached the ears of Cuchullin, the Hero of Ulster, whose friends acclaimed him the greatest warrior in the world. Undefeated he, single-handed, had held up an army; so great was his battle-fury that after a fight three large baths of ice-cold spring water were always prepared for him: when he jumped into the first it went off in steam, when he jumped into the second it boiled over, when he jumped into the third it became a pleasantly hot bath. In fact he was a Great Hero. On hearing that in Skye there lived a woman, unconquered in battle, who offered to teach the heroes of the world how to fight, Cuchullin took two strides from the northern tip of Ireland and landed on Talisker Head; a third stride brought him to Skiach's school in the hills. Here he had expected to be received with awe and honour, and was much peeved to find himself treated as only a 'new boy' and being firmly snubbed all round as a boastful new boy at that. For his fame had not then crossed the seas.

He challenged all the other students to single combat and defeated them. At this Skiach deigned to take notice and gave him permission to fight with her daughter, an honour usually reserved for second-year men. So Cuchullin and Skiach's daughter fought 'for a day and a night and another day' and then, at last, he vanquished her. Great was the wrath of Skiach. She for the first time descended from the high tops to fight. She and Cuchullin fought. They fought for a day and a night and another day, they fought on the mountains and on the moors and in the sea, but neither could come by any advantage. Then Skiach bade all the princes and heroes watch, for never again would they see such a fight. And they fought for a day and a night and another day, but neither gained any advantage.

Then Skiach's daughter was troubled and sent some of her maidens to bring her deer's milk, and she made a cheese from it such as her mother loved, and bade them come and eat. But they would not. So she sent heroes to bring her a deer and she roasted it and called them to come and eat, and it smelt *very* good, but they would not. Then she sent the heroes once again to gather her 'wise' hazel nuts from the trees which grow in the little burns on the side of Broc-Bheinn, and she roasted another deer and stuffed it with roasted hazel nuts and bade them come and eat. And Skiach thought: 'The hazels of knowledge will teach me how to overcome Cuchullin.' And Cuchullin thought: 'The hazels of knowledge will teach me how to overcome Skiach.' So they both came and sat down and ate.

When they tasted the wise hazels they knew that neither could ever overcome the other, so they made peace together and swore that if either called for aid the other would come, 'though the sky fall and crush us'. And Cuchullin returned to Ireland, but not, some say, before Skiach had given him the Firbolg. This strange weapon was forged by the 'little people' in the heart of the mountains and had many magic powers.[1] And Skiach called the mountains where they had fought 'Cuchullin's Hills' ever after.

In due course Skiach passed away and the Cuchullins were alone again. This time an Uraisg, or monster, came to dwell in them. He took up his abode in Coire-nan-Uraisg, the Corrie of the Monster, not far from Loch Coruisk; and here, if you are unfortunate, you may see him, for his grisly shape still haunts it. He was so terrible that no one who saw him ever lived to return and tell of it. Nevertheless he is known to be 'a fearful shape, half human, half goat, with long hair, long teeth, and long curving claws'.

In the Cuchullins, too, though exactly where must not be said, is a cave of gold. Unlike all other treasure caves, there are no barriers here between men and untold wealth. No magic word is required. No fearful monster guards the entrance. He who finds the cave may take as much gold as he needs and return as often as he desires for more, but each time he enters the cave, each time he uses the gold, he will become a little more evil and a little more evil, until he loses his soul. That is the price.

It was not only in prehistoric times that the Cuchullins were a battle-ground. They saw many battles between the Macdonalds and the Macleods. Coire-na-Creiche, the Corrie of the Spoil, for instance, was the scene of a great fight, probably the last formal battle between the two clans. Unfortunately for the Macleods this battle took place in the absence of their chief, Rory Mor, and to this they attribute the Macdonalds' victory.

Loch Coruisk is too well known and has received too many famous visitors (among them Turner, who painted it) to need comment, but it is most often approached by boat from Loch Scavaig. It is, however, a most beautiful

[1] This sounds like a later Scandinavian addition.

walk from Sligachan, down the glen of that name (once, tradition has it, a part of Loch Sligachan), up the Sligachan river, under Marsco's shadow, by Harta Corrie (the scene of another fierce and bloody battle between the Macleods and Macdonalds), and up a steep pass to the crest above Loch Coruisk itself. From the top of this pass there is a most beautiful view of the loch surrounded by mountains; to the east Blaaven (3,042 feet) massive and withdrawn, a strange hill, known as a 'killer' hill and credited with magnetic powers strong enough to disturb compasses.

Sir Walter Scott in his Journal thus describes his visit to the Loch:

Vegetation there was little or none; and the mountains rose so perpendicularly from the water edge, that Borrowdale or even Glencoe, is a jest to them. We proceeded a mile and a half up this deep, dark and solitary lake, which was about two miles long and half a mile broad, and is, as we learned, of extreme depth. The murky vapours which enveloped the mountain ridges, obliged us by assuming a thousand varied shapes, changing their drapery into all sorts of forms, and sometimes clearing off altogether. It is true the mist made us pay the penalty by some heavy and downright showers, from the frequency of which, a Highland boy whom we brought from the farm, told us the lake was popularly called the Water Kettle. The proper name is Loch Corriskin, from the deep Corrie or hollow, in the mountains of Cuillin which affords the basin for this wonderful sheet of water. It is as exquisite a savage scene as Loch Katrine is a scene of romantic beauty. After having penetrated so far as distinctly to observe the termination of the lake under an immense precipice, which rises abruptly from the water, we returned. . . .

In a cave near the loch dwells the ghost of a shepherd who is perpetually engaged in branding the ghost of a sheep, the latter uttering unearthly cries the while.

On Prince Charles Edward's return to Skye from Raasay his guide, Macleod, took the prince to Strath disguised as his servant. They, too, made their way up Glen Sligachan but turned away before Marsco, crossing the ridge between that mountain and Glamaig and so dropping down to the shore of Loch Ainort. And even today a guide is very necessary in the Cuchullins.

Probably no one who has not cultivated land in Skye in some form has the faintest notion of the difficulties to be overcome or the work involved in supporting a family and its beasts on an island croft. The weather is the main difficulty. No agricultural operation *ever* goes uninterrupted. In a place where peat-drying is of the first importance, where the hay harvest may not be in till October and may have to be dried little by little on the fences of the croft at that, and where potatoes are seldom all lifted before December, every fine day and hour in the harvest season is needed if cattle are not to die and children are not to go short of milk in the winter. In the year 1949 Dunvegan's harvest thanksgiving was held on 4 December. Into this carefully planned economy comes, every summer, one (and often more) selfish, conceited, and ignorant tourist, who thinks he knows all about climbing but doesn't. (The real climbers and honest learners are a very different kettle of fish.) But the Ignorant One thinks it clever to go off into the Cuchullins without advice or guide. Then comes the mist or he gets lost or sprains an ankle; next comes the appeal, first to those whose livelihood is guiding: will they give up a day (or several) to search for one who would neither employ nor consult them? And then, if the foolhardy cannot be found, there comes the appeal to the whole island. Buses run from Portree, Dunvegan, Armadale, bringing searchers from them all; bringing men who must decide either to ignore the needs of their own families (and I mean *needs*, not wishes) or else to leave a fellow man to die slowly and horribly in the hills, if he has met with an accident not already fatal.

Is it too much to ask those who do not know the Cuchullins to consult some responsible person before they start? To ask: 'Is the route they propose a good one? Are there any known difficulties to watch for? Is the weather suitable?' And above all to tell their chosen route to someone and stick to what they have arranged. Then, in mist or in case of accident, they can be easily and quickly found without upsetting the harvesting of many townships

4

Sligachan to Portree

———•■•———

Crooked one, dun one,
Little wing grizzled,
Black cow, white cow,
Little bull black-head,
My milch kine have come home,
O dear! that the herdsman would come.

(Herding song of the Portree Braes Fairies)

THIS road should really be traversed for the first time in the opposite direction, Portree to Sligachan, for then its chief attraction, the exciting glimpses of the Cuchullins from near Portree, open out as the road approaches Sligachan until, at a small bridge about half a mile short of the hotel, comes the finest mountain view in Skye, or perhaps in all Scotland. The ten miles of road from Sligachan to Portree consist of ten miles of good, pleasant, but uninspired highway. On the left hand as we near Portree rises Suidh Fhinn, Finn's Seat, 1,367 feet high and with excellent views from its summit of Skye, Raasay, and the Outer Isles. But good as the view from the top undoubtedly is, Finn must have had astonishing sight and voice if he sat there, as traditionally he did, to direct the Fiennes's famous deer drive in Strath.

It is up the slopes of this hill and through the small sea loch below it that the three-mile marathon race is run each year, a special feature of the Portree Games. These Games are held every August on the little peninsula to the south of Portree whose tree-sheltered summit can be seen from the

road. On this headland is one of the loveliest natural amphi-
theatres imaginable, a perfect setting for a Highland
gathering. The headland was first laid out and the Games
started by the 'Dr. Ban' whose many benefactions will not
soon be forgotten. He was anxious to develop Skye's
amenities and was, among other things, the moving spirit
in the draining of Loch Chaluim Chille (see Chapter 7). He
also tried hopefully to make Portree a seaside resort with
a bathing beach and to build a museum and a View Tower
near the Games ground. The View Tower, never completed,
can still be seen there.

Portree, the capital of Skye, is a most attractively situated little town, nestling on the cliff side and looking out
over a beautiful harbour which is also a fine anchorage,
usually well peopled with yachts in the summer season and
sometimes also with warships. The best view of it, as of so
many harbours, is to be had from the sea, but the view from
the town itself is well worth seeing.

The greatest event in Portree's history was the coming
of King James V. Both James IV and James V had been
determined to rule the Hebrides as well as the rest of Scotland and had exerted their authority to that end. In the
year 1540 James V decided to make a Royal Progress to
the north with much impressive pomp and ceremony. In
his entourage was Alex Lindsay, a skilful pilot and naviga-
tor, with orders to chart the till then almost unknown
waters of the Hebrides. The King came with a fleet of
twelve ships and began his visit to Skye by sailing into
Dunvegan Loch. The Castle yielded gracefully to over-
whelming force and Alasdair Crotach, the chief of that
day, with several of his clansmen were carried on board
the King's ship. The fleet sailed on to Score Bay, where
the King is recorded to have been much impressed by the

beauty and strength of Duntulm. The Macdonald chief at that time was a child, the son of Donald Gorm, and James V did not disturb him but sailed on again, to Portree. Here the King himself landed and in his honour his landing-place has ever since been known as Portree (Port an Righ, Port of the King). Before that time the bay was called Loch Columcille after St. Columba, who is believed to have himself built the little chapel whose ruins can still be traced on the small island in the bay which bore his name. In James V's days there were only a few scattered houses, called Kiltarraghan (Talorgan's Cell or Church), where Portree now stands. The King wished to make his headquarters during his visit to Skye on comparatively neutral ground, or at least to avoid the chief centres of Macleods and Macdonalds, so this sheltered but little used anchorage suited him well.

Here, in what is now the Square, he held his court and to him here all the chieftains in Skye came to do homage and vow fealty. These vows, on the whole, they kept well, both to him and to his family, serving the Stuart kings loyally, but they did not think it any part of their duty to keep peace with one another or with other parts of Scotland. As a Macdonald chief wrote to Henry VIII in 1545: 'We have been old enemies to the Realm of Scotland.' Besides the chiefs, the clansmen came on foot and on ponyback from all over the island to see the King in all his power and pomp and all the fine doings at Portree. James held Courts of Justice and settled many disputes: he also enjoyed good sport in the hills. Then the King and his fleet sailed away, carrying Macleod's heir and Norman Clanranald with him as hostages. Not so good. While the King himself had landed at Portree, most of his suite had disembarked a little farther to the east near Scorrybreck Farm, and the rock on which they landed was known ever after as Creag-na-morshluagh, the Rock of the Great Multitude.

Scorrybreck has always been a popular landing-place, especially for those who wished to avoid attracting undue attention, as it is partly screened from Portree by a small rocky headland. The first to discover and make use of this fact were the fairies' cattle. Fairy cattle dwell in the sea but come ashore every day to graze, and the herd which used to graze at Braes always used MacNicol's Rock at Scorrybreck as a landing-place. Each evening the voice of their fairy owner could be heard calling them home, and back to the shore here they would hurry. One day a man took earth from a churchyard and from a molehill and when he heard the fairy calling he flung the earth between the cows and the sea. This they could not pass, and after that they were never able to return to the sea again, so most Skye cattle have fairy blood in them.

MacNicol's Rock next appears in history when Prince Charlie landed there on his return from Raasay and hid in 'Prince Charlie's Cave' (though some say in an old byre near the cave) until it was dark enough for him to start for Strathaird with Macleod.

Between MacNicol's Rock and Prince Charlie's Cave lies another cave, called on the map MacCoitir's Cave after a famous brigand whose headquarters it was for a time and part of whose treasure in gold coins was later discovered near by, but it was better known as the Piper's Cave (see Chapter 15). MacCoitir, or MacCuithen, was a very efficient villain in his day, as the rhyme says:

> *Clan MacCuithen thievish experts,*
> *Clan MacCuithen quick to flatter,*
> *Clan MacVatten theft promoters*
> *Though as small as shaft of dagger.*

He was not the only disturbing element in that district, however, although, to be fair, most of the trouble came from Raasay. A Macleod of Raasay had reason to believe that an unseemly amount of witchcraft was being practised on his island and he set himself to root it out. He was warned of the danger but would not listen, and so in due course he was drowned while crossing the narrow strait between Raasay and Portree Bay by a 'swimming' of small black cats, who climbed into the boat and all over the rigging and sails until all that could be seen as the boat heeled over and sank beneath their combined weight was a purring mass of soft black fur. It is not recorded whether any old women were missed from Raasay after this incident, but perhaps the cats did not drown. Then there is the huge boulder which can be seen on the shore below MacCoitir's Cave. A Raasay man and his wife had a quarrel down on the shore of Raasay and she told him he was only fit to catch whelks, so he picked up this boulder and flung it at her but it missed both her and Raasay and landed on the Skye shore instead. If he was such a bad shot as to miss his mark by a mile or more it does seem to bear out her contention.

To return to 'Town'. From the time of James V onwards Portree was a place of some importance in the island whose capital it now is, and most future guests of importance visited it. To Portree Macdonald of Kingsburgh brought Prince Charles Edward after his night at Kingsburgh. It was in the thatched inn there (now the Royal Hotel) that he said farewell to Flora Macdonald and lay hidden in an upper room waiting for the boat in which Donald Macleod, young Raasay, and his brother were to row him to Raasay and, it was vainly hoped, to safety. In St. Columba's Episcopal Church is a memorial window to Flora Macdonald (see Chapter 7).

Dr. Johnson also dined at the inn on 12 September 1773 on his way from Raasay to Kingsburgh in the rain, and Robert Louis Stevenson was storm-stayed in the Bay. Turner, too, and Tennyson, and Alexander Smith all visited Portree. It is curious now to remember that it was a common subject for discussion among the literary in their day as to which was the greater poet and whose work would live the longer, Tennyson's or Alexander Smith's.

The last visitors of importance to Portree were Queen Elizabeth, the Duke of Edinburgh and Princess Margaret when they visited Skye in 1956.

Portree owes its present importance as chief town and capital of Skye to Sir James Macdonald who, born in 1741, the son of Sir Alex Macdonald (of the '45) and the beloved Lady Margaret, became chief at five years old. He desired to see Portree the centre of Skye and began to build a large village there and a big school, the forerunner of the present High School. As well as fostering education he did all he could to encourage trade to his new town and help local industries. He accomplished much and had he lived might have done much more, but he died at the age of 25 in Rome, leaving behind him the reputation of a good man, a good chief, and a great scholar. By his own wish all his writings were buried with him, so we know less of him today than of many lesser men. His monument is in the church of Kilmore, Sleat. Lord Lyttleton, a college friend, wrote the epitaph.

The names of Portree's streets reflect the Macdonalds' part in her history. 'Somerled Square', for instance, commemorates Somerled, the half-real, half-legendary hero-founder of the Macdonald race. First of the Lords of the Isles and champion of the Celtic cause against the Norse invader, great warrior and able statesman, he is said to have successfully defied and even sailed south to attack Malcolm Canmore, then King of Scotland, and to have been assassinated by Malcolm's friends and buried by Malcolm at his own expense (probably by way of penance) in the sacred soil of Iona. Somerled's somewhat curious manner of obtaining a wife will be found in Chapter 19.

Another case in point is the naming of Wentworth Street. It is called after Godfrey Wentworth, third Lord Macdonald, who made Skye history by eloping to Ireland with the beautiful but illegitimate daughter of a Royal Duke. A most romantic story it is, since neither of them knew her history nor could understand the difficulties placed in the way of their marriage, but one which tangled up the Macdonald inheritance more than all the old battles, feuds, and usurpations ever succeeded in doing.

A fair in honour of St. Maelrubha, one of those who had followed in St. Columba's missionary footsteps in Skye (see Chapter 19), was held at Portree for some centuries, though gradually the name changed into 'Samarive's Fair'. It was held on the first Tuesday in September and must have been a great occasion. One of my uncles had an old nurse, the granddaughter of the last of the Gesto bards, who much amused the children when they teased to know her birthday by saying she was born on 'the Thursday before the Portree Market'. Of course, markets for sheep and cattle are held fairly frequently in Portree on diverse dates, but their elders realized that she meant Samarive's Fair or Market which was used to date by in the old days. She had the most astonishing memory. The first time she ever left Skye was in charge of my uncle when the family were going south. All the way to Inverness in the steamer and the train (the first train she had ever seen) she pointed out every place they passed and told the children its name and history; who had fought whom there, who owned it, how he had acquired it—by marriage or war or purchase—where fairies danced and where water kelpies lived. My grandfather said all her place-names were correct, and her history as far as he knew it, though she knew much that he did not. She could recite almost all her grandfather's repertoire of poems and stories, word for word, he having taught her as a child. My mother often regretted that she did not know enough Gaelic to write them down. The history of the Macleods of Gesto alone, with all their doings, was 'five nights long', which would be about fifteen to twenty-eight hours, I believe, and covered 600 years or more, beginning with a brief résumé of the family's descent from the Norse god Odin! Such memories were common in Skye before reading and writing became so widespread.

NORTH SKYE

Thou who dwellest
In the heights above
O succour us in the depths below;
Vouchsafe to us a day-breeze
As Thou Thyself wouldst wish,
Vouchsafe to us a night-breeze
As we ourselves would choose.
May the clouds hide us,
May the moon shine on the foe,
Be we to windward
And becalmed be they;
O keep firmly tethered
All sudden blasts and accidents—
And leave the rest to us

.   .   .   .   .

And we shall give the glory
To the Trinity and Clement
And the great clerk who lives in Rodel.

(From 'Dunvegan Sea-Hymn'
by Kenneth Macleod)

5

Trotternish: Portree to Flodigarry

Seven herrings are a Salmon's fill,
Seven Salmon are a Seal's fill,
Seven Seals are a Whale's fill,
Seven Whales the fill of a Cirein Croin[1]
And seven Cirein Croin are the fill of the
Big Devil himself.

(From Campbell's *Superstitions of the*
Scottish Highlands and Islands.)

THE peninsula of Trotternish has always been the most fertile and the most fought-for wing of Skye. For it the greatest battle in Skye's history was fought, the Battle of Trouterness, and in it, near Kilmuir, the Norse made their last stand on Blar-a-Bhuailte, Field of the Stricken. No doubt in later times it owed a part of its prosperity to the draining of Loch Chaluim Chille, which resulted in the reclamation of much land so fertile that 'to reap in Monkstadt' became a proverb for receiving riches without labour. For twenty seasons this reclaimed land is said to have produced the heaviest grain harvests in the north, without care or feeding. It became known as 'the granary of Skye, laughing with corn'. But as well as good ground Trotternish has more than its share of the island's few money-making assets. Kilmuir is the centre of Skye's hand-woven tweed industry: Loch Cuithir contains the much-sought-after and rare diatomite, formed from the skeletons of a

[1] Cirein Croin = Sea Serpent.

myriad tiny algae. At the beginning of the century this loch was worked, and the diatomite carried by a sort of tramline to the shore near Inver Tote, where there was a small factory in which it was dried and ground. Then the industry died and the works became derelict; but now once more work is proceeding at Loch Cuithir. Once, too, lime was quarried in the Trotternish hills, to the great benefit of Skye as a whole.

Attractions for the tourist are not lacking either. There is the Quaraing, that frightening rock stronghold; Duntulm, castle and fortress of the Macdonalds of the Isles; Kingsburgh, which sheltered Prince Charlie; and Flodigarry, once the home of Flora Macdonald.

Trotternish is believed to have been heavily wooded until fairly recent times, for the Caledonian Forest included Skye in its kingdom, and it is claimed that there are people now living whose grandparents could remember when the great firs and their accompanying scrub covered large parts of this district. It is said in east Trotternish that eight generations back the cattle could not be seen after they left the yard in the morning until they returned to be milked because of the trees, and that they wore cow-bells like the Swiss cattle do today.

It was in Trotternish, on the shore of Loch Snizort, that St. Columba first landed in Skye in the sixth century (see Chapter 8) and his biographer Adamnan, in his life of St. Columba, records among his miracles one performed here. Near where the saint landed (he says) there was a dense forest, and into this forest Columba went to pray alone and to meditate. As he knelt in prayer he was led to look behind him and perceived a wild boar with its head lowered to charge, rushing to attack him. The saint raised his hand and said: 'Thou shalt proceed no farther in this direction;

perish in the spot which thou hast now reached.' The boar obediently died where it stood.

The most usual way to see the peninsula of Trotternish is to leave Portree by way of Bosville Terrace, with its lovely view over the harbour, and take the road to Storr which follows the valley of the Chracaig river as far as Loch Fada. The first point of interest is the Storr Rock, said to derive its name from Facaill Storach—a buck's tooth—which stands high and commanding to the left of the road about five miles from Portree. Storr is the highest point (2,360 feet) of the long ridge of mountains which form the backbone of Trotternish, and from the top there is a most beautiful view of the Western Mainland—Gairloch, Loch Carron, even the hills of Affaric, are visible on a clear day—and of Skye itself spread out like a map. Storr's black cliff face adds to its grandeur. At its foot stands the 'Old Man of Storr' who, unfortunately, lost his head in a very severe storm half a century ago but is still a stately and impressive pinnacle.

Once, in early medieval times, when the dispute about the date of Easter reached Skye, a priest, dissatisfied with the information to his hand, desired to go to Rome and hear for himself what the Pope had to say about the proper date for Shrove Tuesday. He was a magician. At early dawn he arose and climbed the Storr Rock; there on the brink of the precipice he watched the sun rise and made certain potent spells as it appeared above the earth. These spells not only called up the Devil but transformed him into a horse. The priest leaped on to his back and away to Rome. But the Devil knows a lot about spells and he knew (and the priest knew too) that it was his right to ask what questions he would and the priest must answer them, and answer them truly; yet if the priest mentioned the name of God the magic would be undone, the Devil would vanish in a puff of brimstone and the priest would be left in the sea or in some foreign land, as it might happen. All through that mad ride the Devil propounded questions which required the name of God as an answer, and always the priest answered fully and truly but succeeded in never using the sacred name. So he reached Rome and the Pope in safety, satisfied his conscience as to the proper date to keep Shrove Tuesday, and returned in safety to Skye. How he succeeded in laying the Devil, always the most difficult part of the business, is not known, but tradition has it that the Devil was so greatly impressed by the priest's diabolical cleverness that on being bidden farewell he went quietly, merely replying (in Gaelic): 'Till we meet again.'

The Storr lochs, Loch Fada and Loch Leithan, used to be famous for trout, but now they are the centre of a hydro-electric scheme and a power-station has been built there. It will be interesting to see the reaction of the notorious water-bull, Tot-a-Rom, which inhabits Loch Fada, to this event. The water-horse which used to live in that same loch became a convinced man-killer and was finally killed himself with a knife of pure iron.

Perhaps the strangest tale of these lochs is a true one, the story of the Prince's boat. After Prince Charlie's night at Kingsburgh it was decided that he was no longer safe in Skye; too much was known or guessed about his movements. So young Raasay and his brother, who were in hiding near Portree, were approached and offered him shelter in Raasay. But the question was how to get him there. They had no boat and dared not borrow or steal one for fear its absence should put the redcoats on the Prince's track. But they were boys of resource. They bethought them of a small rowing-boat which was always kept on

Loch Fada. This boat they took and, although one of them was but half-recovered from a wound, they carried it two miles to the cliff-top and then somehow got it down the cliff to the sea undamaged, and so to Raasay to fetch a boat large enough to be safe for the Prince, and a trustworthy crew to row it. The absence of the loch boat was noticed by some troops (who wanted trout for supper) and they reported it to their officer, who merely inquired coldly if they thought the boat had wings and the fugitive had flown off in it, since by no other means could a small boat on an inland loch have been of use to get him out of Skye.

After passing the Storr lochs the road, roughly following the coastline, passes many a dun and waterfall while a whole series of beautiful views unfold themselves. Off the coast, not far from where the Bearseraig river leaves Loch Leithan and runs out to sea, lies the tiny island of Holm; this, with Fladda Island, was once believed to be Tir-nan-h'oig, the Land of Perpetual Youth, the Celtic Paradise. When this coast road was being made the workmen found, 'opposite Holm Island', a large underground passage or dwelling, built of stone and stone-roofed. About fifty yards of this passage was explored and the bones of prehistoric animals were found in it, also some flint weapon-heads. The explorers believed that the passage continued for some distance beyond the spot they reached. It was also found that in parts the apparently solid earth was held up on a series of limestone arches over caverns.

On the shore, about three miles beyond Storr itself, stands a huge boulder with a strange hole in it, in shape like the door of a church, so that it was known as Eaglais Bhreagach, or False Church. Here, it is said, the famous robber chief, MacCoitir, performed the rite of Taghairm (roasting live cats to raise the Devil) and persuaded the Devil (for he was very fair of speech) to grant plenty for life to him and to all his band. The Devil, as usual, kept his promise, but eventually carried the whole band off to hell with the exception of MacCoitir himself. MacCoitir he could not touch, for he had once done a good deed and so was given a chance of repentance. But MacCoitir wished to rejoin his comrades and when the Devil refused to have him he threatened to take hell by storm could he but find a sword which would not melt: a favourite threat, it seems. It is said that, having refused heaven and been rejected by hell, he still walks the moors of Trotternish.

It was at Bearreraig, a little farther down the coast, that the rite of Taghairm is believed to have been performed for the last time, in this case to learn the future.

The next point of interest is Lonfearn. Here 'Kingsburgh' lay hidden for some time after sheltering the Prince. The old house of Lonfearn, with its walls five feet thick, belonged for many generations to a cadet branch of the Nicolsons of Scorrybreck. They, it is said, received it from a Macdonald of Sleat, to be held rent free 'while a wave strikes the shore or a black cow has milk'. This clan, the Nicolsons of Scorrybreck, were by tradition the oldest clan in Skye. They were reputed to have received Duirinish, Assynt, and other lands including Scorrybreck from Malcolm Canmore for saving a great herd of cattle from the Norsemen in their native Sutherland. If this is correct they were then known as Macryul or Macryal. John, the seventeenth and last, left Scorrybreck for Tasmania. The last of the direct line known in Skye was Sheriff Nicolson, who died in 1893 in Edinburgh. He wrote the beautiful song to Skye which begins:

My heart is yearning for thee, O Skye,
Dearest of Islands.

An old Gaelic saying is: 'Clann Mhicneacail a' Brochan,
Bithidh an t'uisge ann air latha am posaidh' (Nicolsons of
the porridge, there will be rain on their marriage day).
But why?

From here the road runs on, by the townships of Breckrey and Culnaknock, to Loch Mealt, guarded by its ring of
duns, Dun Bearg, Dun Raisaburgh, Dun Grianan, and, a
little farther to the south, Dun Connavern. One wonders
why Loch Mealt was so precious. Dun Bearg is said to have
been one of the 'Fire Hills' whose beacon called the clans
to arms and to have been last so used in the '45.

One Maol-Moire MacInnes once lived in Breckrey and of
him the following tale was told. While serving under Marl-
borough in the Low Countries he went forward with a
young officer and a few other men to reconnoitre. Accidentally they surprised a fairly large party of the enemy round
a wine-shop and had no difficulty in capturing them. Then
arose the question of what to do with them. To shoot them
in cold blood was repugnant, to let them go was to give the
alarm,,while to take them back to headquarters would require the whole strength of the little company. The matter
had reached a deadlock when MacInnes offered to take
them back single-handed if the officer would first form all
the prisoners up into line with their backs turned and their
hands in the air. His offer was accepted. He then walked
down the line cutting each man's braces. As he anticipated,
custom proved strong and he had no trouble during the
march, every man being entirely occupied holding up his
trousers!

Next comes the township of Elishader, with near it, on
the coast, the famous Kilt Rock. Then the road crosses the
Kilmartin river. Close to the bridge another road takes off
to the left, to the townships of Marishader and Garros.

Marishader was long the home of the Martins of Marishader, famous in Skye history. Martin Martin, whose book on Skye, written in 1716, is still much read, was one of this family. Standing on the moor near Garros are two pillars of unpolished stone. They mark the site and point the moral where two foolish brothers fought to the death for an inheritance.

The main road passes on round beautiful Staffin Bay with its townships: first Staffin itself, where a Martin of Marishader built as its inn the first slated house in Trotternish, which daring innovation brought much custom; then Stenscholl, Brogaig, Glashvin, and Digg. Near Stenscholl is the steading where once, long ago, one Airidh Mhic Iain Ghill, going at dusk to milk his cows, found a strange beast sheltering with them. He whistled up his dogs but the beast spoke and begged him to call them off. This he refused to do, whereupon it fled, with the dogs in pursuit. Next morning all his dogs were found mangled on a point near by, since called the Promontory of the Blue Hounds. Near Stenscholl, too, is a mineral spring which is said to have healing properties as great as those of Strathpeffer. At Brogaig another road takes off to the left and after passing the old Kilmartin burial-ground runs up to the Quaraing and down on the farther side into Uig. A strange story is told about this old Kilmartin graveyard (the burial-place of the Martin family). Very long ago there was a little church on the Garafad slope and it was decided to lay out a graveyard round it. Men were engaged and set to work. When night fell they left their tools tidily stacked beside their digging and went home. Next morning they found all their work undone and their tools missing. These were later discovered on the river bank. The men took back their tools, very angry at this foolish joke as they thought it, and began work again. That night the same thing occurred, and the next night and the next. At last the angry workmen decided to keep watch all night. They did so. It was a night 'in the dark of the moon' but clear and starry; they saw nothing, they heard nothing, yet in the morning their tools were again missing, their work again undone. Then they realized that some power not of this world was opposing their efforts and that the constant removal of all tools to one spot might be in the nature of a broad hint. They took the hint and began to lay out a burial ground on that spot, which is now the old graveyard of Kilmartin. As soon as work was begun here all interference stopped and the work prospered.

The Quaraing itself, obviously the result of some great natural upheaval, has been so often described, and its famous 'Needle Rock' so often photographed that further description seems unnecessary. But its atmosphere can never be captured. Perhaps it can best be summed up by saying that it is as if 'the terror that walketh in darkness' here walks by day.

There are, as far as I know, no particular legends or stories about the Quaraing. 'The Cup' was used as a safe hiding-place for cattle in time of trouble because two or three men could hold the entrance against a force; and there was, of course, a spectre, but it was laid by throwing a knife through it. Apart from that there is a singular dearth of legend. It seems almost as if something so horrible, or else so wicked, had taken place here that the survivors (if any) never dared to speak of it and so it blessedly passed from human memory. But the earth and the rocks remember.

I have been told by two men, both well accustomed to the loneliness of moor and mountain and both constitutionally incapable of believing in 'haunts' or seeing ghosts, that the Baca Ruach, the back of this same range of hills, which they visited at different times, gives just this same feeling of terror and of potent, living evil. All other Skye hills are friendly, but not the Baca Ruach. 'Anything might live there.'

Let us return once more to the coast road. After passing round Staffin Bay it runs through pleasant country and gives a good view of Flodigarry Island. Once there lived on this island an old man called Iain Ruadh and his daughter Mairi, who kept house for him. He had a herd of black cattle and the pride of his heart was his great black bull. Now, on the mainland opposite there lived (among others) a boy, Allan, who loved Mairi dearly, but her father did not want to part with her. Who would keep house for him if she went? So he not only forbade her to see young Allan but let it be known that should she ever marry, no dowry would accompany her, no, not so much as a calf unless so be it had slit ears. This was the crowning of it, for a slit-eared calf meant one whose father was a Tarbh Uisge, or water-bull, and such calves should always be killed at birth, otherwise they bring disaster to the herd. Now at this time the whole township of Flodigarry was being terrorized and ruined by just such a water-bull. Every night it came out of the water—what water no man knew for none dared watch for it or follow it, but some said Loch Fada—but wet it undoubtedly was, for its great dripping form had once been seen in the moonlight. And each night from sunset to sunrise, so the people said, it ate and it ate and it ate. Such part of their crops as it did not eat it trampled under foot. They dared not fence lest the creature should take it as a personal insult, and woe betide him who offends the Mighty Ones of the lochs. So ruin stared the township in the face, and at the mention of a split-eared calf Allan's father naturally became as set against the marriage of his son and Mairi as old Iain Ruadh himself.

But the young couple were determined not to be separated. Every evening Mairi slipped out of her father's house down to the shore, and every evening young Allan swam across the water to visit her. One night, as she waited, she heard a commotion in the sea and much splashing and then she heard her name called in a faint voice. She hurried down to the water's edge, then out into the breaking surf to help Allan, completely exhausted, ashore. When he had recovered sufficiently to talk he told her how, when halfway across, he had heard splashing and snorting close to him and had seen, making towards him, a huge monster; 'its head was black as the thunder cloud, its nostrils redder than the lightning, from its great bull neck it shook the waves as they broke', and the noise it made so terrified him, Allan admitted, that he had swum until he was exhausted. They agreed that he must have met the deadly Tarbh Uisge. Mairi was terrified for him and rather than that he should again cross the path of the Mighty One, she promised that the following night, if he could find a boat, she would elope with him. This he promised to do. The following night, helping himself to a convenient boat, he rowed over to fetch Mairi. But half-way across he heard again the splashing and stertorous breathing; he rested on his oars so as to attract no undesirable attention, and watched. Through the water, passing close by the boat and puffing like a grampus, came the monster. And he was none other than the great black bull of the island herd, who crossed to the mainland nightly for a really good feed of unfenced corn! Allan, perhaps wisely, decided to tell Mairi nothing of his discovery, fearing that she might be less willing to fly with him from her pet bull than from a sea monster.

Perhaps also he felt some gratitude to the bull. Anyhow, it was not until many years later, when 'Mr. and Mrs. Allan', a very happy couple, returned from Australia that the secret of the water-bull was told.

Flodigarry House itself is chiefly known as being for a time the home of Flora Macdonald after her marriage to 'Young Kingsburgh' and before Kingsburgh itself became theirs. The present house, in its pleasant wooded grounds with a lovely view, was enlarged and to a great extent rebuilt by descendants of hers, the Livingstone Macdonalds. Unfortunately that branch of the family died out and the house is now an hotel. Not far from the house is a small mound and so green is its grass that none can doubt the fairies dance there. Indeed, their music has often been heard: once, a man joined them in the dance and disappeared, but was rescued when, exactly one year later, his brother flung a knife so that it stuck in his clothing. He believed he had only danced for an hour.

Near Flodigarry House, and not far from the shore, are two wells. Once there was only one spring here and from it the people of the township drew their water. But in those days the people in this district were some of them Christian and some of them pagan and, as one would expect, they quarrelled. Most fiercely of all they quarrelled over the well, each faction trying to prevent the other from using it. At this time there lived on Flodigarry Island a very wise old hermit, St. Turog, and the people, both pagan and Christian, appealed to him to settle, once for all, the dispute over the well. The saint agreed to meet them at the spring (a great concession) and hear both stories. But the recounting of their supposed rights and grievances worked both sides up to such a pitch of fury that, forgetting what was seemly in the presence of the saint, they fell upon one another with fists and stones, whereupon the old man, very angry, struck the well with his staff and it became dry. He then returned to the island.

Days passed and at last a very subdued deputation waited upon St. Turog. They would do anything he told them, perform any penance, if he would but return their spring, they said, and in future they would share good gifts equally. St. Turog allowed himself to be rowed ashore once more. All the township awaited him. He refused to reopen the well but remained near the shore, bidding the people separate before him, Christians to the one hand and pagans to the other, by two staff lengths. Then he struck the ground, first in front of one party, then in front of the other, and where his staff had touched the earth two springs, crystal clear, gushed up. Some say, however, that he bade each party, as a penance, dig for many days where he had pointed, and that water appeared on the third day.

The people were delighted and surrounded the old man with shouts of joy. Then he bade them, lest they forget their folly, to go sunwise round each well on the first day of each month before filling their vessels and drop into the well an offering of gratitude for the water. This they promised to do ever after. The two springs sometimes overflow into the rock pools below. Where the one overflows can still be found holy relics, sacred medals and little carved crosses; below the other the finds are quite different, being beads, carved shells, and curios; but below both are small coins.

6

Trotternish: Duntulm

———◆■◆———

*Spiced with anecdotes of prison cells and the torture
chamber.*

(*The Yeomen of the Guard*, W. S. Gilbert)

AFTER leaving Flodigarry the road, a very good one,
turns inland across the head of the peninsula. It runs
through the townships of Kilmoluag and Solitote and
passes not far from Shulista, which was the land of the
hereditary doctors to the Macdonalds, the Macleans of
Shulista. Then, near Duntulm Lodge, now an hotel, Duntulm itself appears upon its cliff, silhouetted against sky
and sea, still black and forbidding, its ruins defying the
Hebridean storms with the same grim determination with
which the ancient castle once defied men. It stands lonely,
a place of ghosts and bloodshed and unhappy memories.

Duntulm first appears in history (or legend) as Dun
Dhaibidh, said to have been an ancient Pictish fort which
got its name from a Viking who seized it in the early days
of the Norse invasion from its Celtic owner who had, himself, dislodged its original garrison. The Lord of the Isles
later drove out the Norsemen, seized the dun, and built a
new and improved fort there. It is difficult to understand
how such an extraordinarily strong-looking cliff fort could
have been seized so often. Was it treachery? Or want of a
good well? Or, as some said, a curse? Be that as it may,
Duntulm soon changed hands again and became the property of the Macleods. But in the sixteenth century the

Macdonalds of Sleat, in the troublous times which followed the Battle of Bloody Bay, seized both Trotternish and Duntulm. The Macleods drove them out again in due course, but the Macdonalds, as was their custom, soon returned. This time they not only seized Trotternish but drove the whole population before them across the Snizort river and out of the peninsula, partly, no doubt, because the people belonged to or owed fealty to Clan Macleod, but partly also because the Macdonalds were early exponents of the scorched-earth policy. The two clans in arms and the fugitives all met near the mouth of the Snizort river and here on the moor the Battle of Trouterness, sometimes called the last real battle in Skye, was fought (see Chapter 8). It ended in a victory for Donald Gorm, who then took up his residence at Duntulm, turning it from a fort into a castle. The exact date on which Duntulm became the chief dwelling-place of the Macdonalds of Sleat is not known, but it was about 1539.

The early history of Duntulm is confusing because Donald Gorm, the first chief to make it his official residence, was succeeded by his son Donald Gorm, sometimes called Donald Gormson, who was succeeded by his son Donald Gorm, generally called Donald Gorm Mor, who was succeeded by his nephew Donald Gorm, who is sometimes, but, alas, not often, referred to as Donald Gorm Og. However, the first Donald Gorm began immediately to make great improvements to the fort: to show the trouble that was taken it is remembered that 'earth from seven kingdoms' was imported to lay out the gardens and policies. Undoubtedly for a time Duntulm was a wonderful castle. James V, who sailed into Score Bay when the chief, Donald Gormson, was a child, declared himself much impressed alike by its great strength, its size, and its beauty.

Below the castle, deep grooves can be seen in the rocks; these are reputed to have been worn by the keels of the Macdonald galleys when drawn up on the shore. Donald Gorm died late in 1539 and can never have seen his plans completed. His son, Donald Gormson, did much to raise the prestige of the clan; but he, in turn, was succeeded by a child, his son Donald Gorm Mor.

Donald Gorm Mor was chief in most troubled times, and not the least of his troubles was his cousin Hugh, Uisdean Mac Gillespic Chleirich, who had more than once plotted his murder as well as murdering others and also plunging the clan into an unwanted war. Hugh built himself a fortress, Castle Uisdean, without doors or windows, its only entrance being through the roof, and, when it was completed, wrote to Donald Gorm Mor inviting him to a house-warming. He also wrote to one Martin from East Trotternish, a mean rogue, setting out in detail just how Martin was to murder the chief during the house-warming when he would be Hugh's guest, also what reward he might expect. Having written the two letters and sealed them up in separate packets, Hugh unfortunately confused them and sent the flowery invitation to Martin and the plans for his murder to Donald Gorm Mor. Very tactless. Not unnaturally, Donald Gorm Mor was much annoyed and sent men to seize Hugh. The result was a long siege of Hugh's castle, which ultimately fell, chiefly through starvation and efforts to get food to the garrison which gave away the only safe path through the bog surrounding it. Hugh disguised himself as a woman servant and sat querning corn, but his great size betrayed him and after a fierce struggle he was carried prisoner to Duntulm. Here he was imprisoned in a dungeon and fed on salt meat and salt fish without water until he died, mad with thirst. His screams and curses are

The Quaraing Pass. Showing the old road from Staffin to Uig

said to echo through the castle to this day. For Duntulm is much haunted.

The next interesting event was the hand-fasting of Margaret, sister of Rory Mor Macleod of Dunvegan, to Donald Gorm Mor for a year. Donald Gorm Mor appears to have been a rather unpleasant man (and an even more unpleasant ghost!). He took a dislike to the unfortunate Margaret because she had lost an eye, treated her with contempt, and finally returned her to her brother mounted on a one-eyed horse, escorted by a one-eyed man, and followed by a one-eyed dog. One wonders rather anxiously how he found all three so conveniently. This insult, needless to say, resulted in a fresh outbreak of clan fighting, called 'Cogadh na Cailliche Caime', the War of the One-eyed Woman. The weeping of the unhappy Margaret can still, it is said, be heard at Duntulm.

Donald Gorm Mor had three wives but no son to succeed him, so at his death Duntulm passed to his nephew Donald Gorm Og, but without certain most important parchments. Donald Gorm Og, in fact, had a really poor time at first; without the lost papers his position was most insecure and, moreover, neither he nor his household could get any sleep owing to the noise made nightly by the ghost of Donald Gorm Mor and two friend-ghosts of his who came every night and drank themselves drunk in the castle. In the early stages of the night Donald Gorm Mor could be heard singing:

> *I was in Edinburgh last night,*
> *I am in my own mansion tonight,*
> *And worth of mote in the sunbeam*
> *I have not in me of might.*

Later, the three would become more noisy and violent. At

length Donald Gorm Og consulted a priest, who blessed seven torches of pine-wood and bade him take them, with six men whom he could trust, and, when the drunken orgy was at its height, confront his uncle. This he did and the ghost, impressed by the sacred flames, not only promised quieter and more circumspect visits in future, but also told his nephew where he had concealed the much-needed papers.

Later comes the tragic story of the little heir, less than a year old, who fell from his nurse's arms on to the rocks below his nursery window and was killed. His baby cry can still be heard, it is said, as can the cries of the terrified nurse when the Macdonald of the day, overcome with rage at his son's death, ordered her to be bound and set adrift on the sea in a leaking boat. His men dragged her away, shrieking and sobbing, but only, it is believed, to hide her in a dungeon until they could smuggle her safely back to her parents' croft near Treaslane, a dummy meanwhile being sent out to sea. Nevertheless, her frenzied cries are thought still to haunt Duntulm. So, too, do footsteps, curses, and groans which issue from the long-empty dungeons of the castle.

These are, as one might say, the personal ghosts, but besides that, at sunset or soon after, especially if the evening be misty, a procession of kilted warriors dressed in many different tartans can be seen, all fully armed and parading as if ready for battle, close to the castle. Some say that these are the ghosts of the many who fell before its walls. But once the evening mists saw a more substantial, though less warlike, army, for Donald Gorm Mor is said on one occasion, when hard pressed by the Macleods, who had surprised the castle with the garrison absent, to have acted on his fool's advice and turned out maids and scullions and his few remaining men-at-arms to march round the castle in an endless 'crocodile' to give the impression of a great army entering its gates. The knoll which made this manœuvre possible is still known as the knoll of the Round and Round, Cnoc a Roladth, though others say that its name came from malefactors being rolled down it in a nail-studded barrel.

Close to Duntulm, too, is Ru Meanish, the Hill of Pleas, where justice was done, and Cnoc a Chrochaidh, the Knoll of the Hanging, where sentences were carried out until Black John of Garrafad, when about to be hanged, carried off the gallows by supernatural agency, the Devil having given him these powers for a year and a day. When the agreed time was up, Black John was to give himself up to the Evil One. In due course Satan arrived to claim his bargain. 'There I am', said John of Garrafad, pointing to his shadow, and the Devil (surely a very simple Devil) happily carried it off. John never cast a shadow again but did well enough without one.

The Macdonalds last fought as a clan at Sheriffmuir in 1715, when they came out in support of the Jacobite cause. Before they left the island a great ball was held in the castle: it was the last festivity to be held at Duntulm and many tales are told of it (see Chapter 9). At it an old woman weaving in the castle was called upon by Sir Donald Macdonald, 'Donald of the War', to sing to the company. She sang an ancient weaving song and from this 'detailed description in verse' Sir Donald 'revived the pattern of tartan cloth worn by Donald of Harlaw'.

As a result of their participation in the Rising the Macdonald lands were declared forfeit in 1716, and Skye tradition makes the family leave Duntulm in that year for Monkstadt, never to return; but Duntulm is still mentioned as their residence in an account of the Highland Clans published in 1725. What happened after the forfeiture is variously told: *The History of Skye*, by Alexander Nicolson, says the forfeited estate was sold by the Government in 1723 and bought by the tenants for Macdonald again for £21,000, which remained a mortgage upon the estate; Alexander Mackenzie in his *History of the Macdonalds*, however, says that the property forfeited in 1715 was given to William Taighter, 'a brother' of Sir Alexander Macdonald (who succeeded Sir Donald) and that he returned it all to his brother and chief except the farm of Aird, just north of Duntulm, where he lived out his life, and also the Island of Valley, for which his descendants paid a yearly rental of one shilling. William had a great funeral and was buried near Flora Macdonald.

Near Duntulm lies the headland of Bornaskitaig. A Trotternish tradition makes this the scene of the well-known legend of the Macdonald crest, the hand holding a dagger. More usually this is told of an island. The Macdonalds and Macleods both claimed or desired this promontory, and it was decided that each clan should bring their best war galley and race for it, the winner being he whose hand should first touch the land. The Macleod galley was winning when young Macdonald rose to his feet, struck off his left hand with his dagger and flung it ashore. Macdonald then claimed that a Macdonald hand, his son's, was the first to touch the earth, so the land was his. The Macleods agreed.

In Duntulm Bay lies Tulm Island and beyond it, in clear weather, Fladdachuan, Fladda of the Ocean, can be seen. In olden times this was a sacred spot, held by many to be Tir-nan-Og, the Isle of Perpetual Youth, which lay in the west; here it is always summer and the sun never sets. The puffins recognized its sacred nature and never began any venture until they had circled the island three times sunwise; this they did also on arriving in Skye and before leaving it. It was held by some to be the reason why in Skye people used to turn three times sunwise before starting a new enterprise. The Druids held it in veneration and St. Columba caused a chapel to be built there. On its altar lay a black stone which some say was the original altar stone of the Druids and which was known as the Weeping Stone because it was always wet. Until fairly recently fishermen used to land on the island and pour three handfuls of sea water on the stone to procure favourable winds or to stop bad floods. The Weeping Stone no longer exists, or at least is no longer to be found where the altar once stood.

The story is told of a fisherman who had perpetual bad luck at the fishing until he was on the brink of ruin. At last he decided to visit Fladdachuan, pour water on the stone, and pray for favourable wind and good catches. But his usual luck followed him, for his boat was only a small one and on the way across what should appear, close by, but a large whale, which overturned it with a flip of its tail? Clinging to the upturned keel the fisherman cried to St. Columba for help. Instantly, so he told on his return, a white figure appeared on the water beside him and gently rebuked the whale for its clumsiness in overturning the boat, and especially a boat on pilgrimage to Fladdachuan, and bade it as a penance push man and boat safely to the island. This the whale duly did. Such were the fisherman's catches after this event that his good luck became proverbial.

7

Trotternish: Duntulm to Portree

Let not Thy grace fall upon us as the water on the back of the goose, unabiding.

(Old Trotternish prayer)

AFTER Duntulm the road runs along the coast as far as the township of Osmigarry; here a loop-road takes off inland, serving the townships of Peinduin and Heribusta, and close to the junction of these roads lies the old graveyard of Kilmuir.

The earliest parish church of Kilmuir was that of Kilmoluag, dedicated to St. Moluac and giving its name to the Kilmoluag river on whose banks it stood. It was succeeded by the church of Kilmhairi, which remained in use until long after the Reformation. Indeed, the skull and thigh-bones of Uisdean MacGillespic Chleirich, famous for his great size, were said to be on view on the window ledges of that church until 1827, it being the custom in Skye at one time to display the skull and bones of those who had died, to remind men of their latter end. But now no trace of the church remains except its ancient burial-ground. The present church is quite modern.

This old graveyard saw many a great funeral in its time, including Flora Macdonald's, which was by far the largest ever known in Skye, and here her memorial, a modern Celtic cross, is to be seen. On it are engraved Dr. Johnson's words: 'A name that will be mentioned in history and, if

courage and fidelity be virtues, mentioned with honour.'
In this burial-ground, too, there are some early medieval
carved tombstones like those in Iona. The history of one is
known, at least traditionally.

It marks the grave of Angus Gille Martin, the first member of the Martin family to settle in Skye. He got his Gaelic
name of Aonghas na Gaoithe from his wandering life, for he
was a seafarer, visiting all the Western Isles in turn in his
galley in all weathers and at all seasons. Tradition has it
that he was a famous warrior in his youth and fought in the
wars of Sorley Buy Macdonald in Ireland, then took to the
sea, and later married a Danish princess, Biurnag or Bere-
nice, had seven sons, and settled in Trotternish. Over his
grave is a stone carved to represent a recumbent warrior,
which he himself brought from Iona. Whether the other
similarly incised and carved stones to be found in all the
older Skye graveyards were also brought from Iona or are
local copies no one now remembers, but in this connexion
it is interesting to note the story given in *The Macleods
of Dunvegan* that the family of MacAskell were Constables
of Dunscaith in the early days when it was a Macleod fortress, were Macleod of Macleod's lieutenants both by land
and sea, commanding both troops and birlinns (galleys),
and that on one occasion one of them served the clan so well
that Macleod of Macleod decreed that 'whenever a Mac-
Askell was buried, a monumental stone, having a warrior
in full armour with the proper emblems of the Clan cut
upon it, should be put up over his grave'. In almost every
churchyard throughout the Isles these are still to be seen.
The stones were carved by the monks of Iona, who worked
in a cave in the Ross of Mull and sold their work for the
good of the Church.

But enough of graveyards. Down the road to the left lies

Peinduin , once the hereditary property of the Macdonalds'
pipers, the MacArthurs. Here they, like the MacCrimmons
in Borreraig, had a piping college and their pupils practised
the pipes on Cnoc Phail, a small hillock near by. The college
of Peinduin never became as famous as Borreraig, however; indeed, there is a record of one MacArthur paying a
cow to MacCrimmon as entrance fee for his son to the Mac-
Crimmon college. On the coast not far from here is the
famous Cave of Gold, 'Uamh Oir', in which was hidden a
hoard or 'pot' of pure gold, guarded by a terrible monster.
This creature came farther and farther afield in search of
food, harrying the whole countryside. At last the Mac-
Arthur of the day felt that it was laid upon him to enter
the cave and deal with the beast. He said farewell to his
family and, with pipes skirling (and an audience watching
from a safe distance!) he entered the cave. Here is a translation of the chant that he was playing:

> *I shall come never, return never;*
> *Ere I return from the Cave of Gold*
> *The kidling flocks will be goats of the rocks*
> *And the children weak will be warriors bold.*
> *I am woe, woe, under spells to go;*
> *I'll be for aye in the Cave of Gold.*

The listeners heard his pipes beneath the ground, then the
tune changed and broke, there were sounds as of a conflict,
fierce and terrible, and then these words were heard in
Gaelic:

> *Pity me, without hands three,*
> *Two for the pipes and a sword hand free.*

MacArthur, as he had foretold, never returned, but he
achieved his purpose, for the monster was never seen again
and the people of Kilmuir lived in peace.

The main road runs on through the many townships of Kilmuir, for this is a rich district. The flat land now lying between it and the sea was once the famous Loch of Chaluim Chille. In the days of St. Columba (after whom it was called) this was a veritable loch, containing in its centre a little island still marked on the maps as Eilean Chaluim Chille. Here the saint founded a small chapel and a tower, believed to have been placed there first for safety in a pagan world, but to have become the centre from which Christianity spread over Skye. That St. Columba himself ever lived there is doubtful, but the ruins of a cluster of beehive cells show that it must have been a community of some size at an early date. A monastery was also founded there, though at a rather later time, and at Kilvaxter, near the loch, was a chapel and foundation under the rule of the Nuns of Iona. In later times the island was the refuge of Norse pirates (see Chapter 15). Later still the loch lost much of its water and became a great marsh. From 1715 onwards attempts were made to drain and use part of this marshland, but it was not until 'The Doctor Ban' (Dr. Alexander Macleod) undertook the matter in 1825 that a proper outlet to the sea was dug and the whole loch was drained and became the richest arable land in Skye. Ever since, Monkstadt has been known as the granary of Skye. The richness of its soil gave rise to many proverbs. For twenty years it bore crops of both barley and oats without manure. The Macleods in envy christened it the 'Country of the Stappacks' (meal and water) and the Macdonalds replied by calling Duirinish the 'Country of the Footless Stockings'.

Monkstadt itself was the house to which the Macdonalds moved from Duntulm and it was to Monkstadt that Flora Macdonald went to arrange plans with Lady Margaret for

Prince Charlie's safety. It was near here, on the coast, that Prince Charlie and Flora landed and, indeed, even today the country from Monkstadt to Kingsburgh is Prince Charlie country, full of memories of the Prince and of Flora Macdonald.

Flora was visiting her brother at Milton, in Uist, in the summer of 1746 when the Prince sought refuge in that island. The hunt was closing in and his danger was great, so his friends felt that he should leave Uist as his presence there was suspected. But how? It was at this point that the plan for his escape as Flora's maid was first put forward; by whom has never been known officially but it is believed that the unlikely happened and the plan was suggested and made possible by her stepfather, Hugh Macdonald, who, though no Jacobite and in fact commanding the Royalist levies in the island, did not want the Prince captured. Flora met the Prince, Captain O'Neill, and Neil MacEachan in the Shieling of Alisary at Milton and refreshed them with drinks of buttermilk, for it was hot and sultry. The plan was then explained to her and she immediately refused to play her part, giving as her reason that the Macdonalds of Kingsburgh were her good friends and she could not bring such danger upon them. She added, too, that she would lose her good name. Captain O'Neill at once offered to marry her by oath, Scotch fashion, there and then. This she refused. There seems little doubt that as Flora became engaged to Allan Macdonald of Kingsburgh not long after her release, and with few further meetings between them, she must have loved him already. The one poem we have of hers shows how deeply. What she was in fact being asked to do was to bring the danger of death to his parents and of confiscation to his home; also it seemed probable that he would hear most undesirable tales of her adventures, for in those days modest, gently bred girls did not career about the country in the company of adventurers, even princely ones. To make it worse, Allan was serving in the Royalist forces, in which he held a commission.

Flora's refusal caused another plan to be put forward; this was that the Prince should go to Hugh Macdonald of Baleshare in North Uist (a cousin of Flora's, and a Jacobite) and hide there. But Hugh Macdonald refused to accept the responsibility, on the ground of the danger being too great. That was too much for Flora and she agreed to try to smuggle Prince Charlie into Skye as her maid, but refused to allow Captain O'Neill to be of the party as he could not pass as a Highlander. Then she and Lady Clanranald hastily made 'Betty Burke's' trousseau. This consisted of a calico gown, sprigged with blue, a light-coloured quilted petticoat, a mantle of dun camelot 'made after the Irish fashion' with a hood, a cap, broad apron, shoes, and stockings. It was when he changed into women's clothes that he presented Flora with his shoe buckle. Flora's stepfather, as officer commanding troops in Uist, gave her a letter of safe-conduct, saying he wished her to return to her mother's house in these troublous times, and to travel escorted by Neil MacEachan and accompanied by her Irish maid, Betty Burke. He also gave her a letter to carry to her mother, his wife, explaining the somewhat uncouth Irish maid's reputed skill as a spinster and bidding her keep her or not as she wished!

The party set off in an open boat and were caught by storm off Ardmore Point. They tried to land there but were fired on by soldiers desirous of making them heave to, so rowed on. For a time they sheltered in a cave in Waternish Head, then crossed the mouth of Loch Snizort and landed Flora near Monkstadt to wait upon Lady Margaret Mac-

donald, a staunch Jacobite who had had much to do with
Flora's upbringing. Here she hoped to get news of troop
movements. Meanwhile the boat passed farther down the
coast to 'Prince Charlie's Point', where 'Betty Burke' remained and settled himself to wait with such patience as he
could muster. Meanwhile Flora had reached Monkstadt
and found Royalist troops there; she managed to give her
news to Lady Margaret, however, and then the two ladies
set themselves to charm the officer-in-charge that he might
suspect nothing. Lady Margaret gave the news to Macdonald of Kingsburgh who, for some time, had managed
the Macdonald estates for her husband, and he smuggled
food and instructions to the waiting fugitive by Neil Mac-
Eachan. Some time after dinner, which must have strained
their social gifts to the uttermost, Flora Macdonald rose
and, saying she wished to reach Kingsburgh before nightfall in these disturbed days, she took her departure. The
officer concerned offered his company, and a troop as a
guard, but she assured him that her Irish maid and an
escort awaited her and were sufficient protection. All went
well until they reached the Hinnisdal river, where 'Betty
Burke' raised his skirts so high when fording it that a boy
who saw was amazed and rushed home to tell of the 'wild
Irish girl', while Flora and 'Kingsburgh' anxiously up-
braided the Prince, who only laughed and insisted on
stopping to drink from what has ever since been known
as 'Prince Charlie's Well'.

At last they reached the shelter of Kingsburgh House,
and thankful they were. Mrs. Macdonald was in bed when
they arrived, for it was late, and her daughter Anne rushed
up to her room, full of Flora's arrival and of her gawky
Irish maid, whom, said Anne, her father treated 'with
more respect than ever he shows Flora'. She was quickly

followed by 'Kingsburgh' with news of their guest. Then all was excitement and bustle in the old house; dry clothes for the Prince, the best linen and a warming-pan for his bed, and, by no means least important, the brewing of brandy punch in the best punch-bowl. And thereby hangs a tale.

'Kingsburgh' knew well he was suspected of being a possible host to the Prince: was there not Sir Alexander's letter to prove it? (see Chapter 18). It was therefore decided that the royal guest must spend no more than one night under his roof. An early start, before tongues could wag, was imperative. Therefore, said 'Kingsburgh', we must go easy on brandy punch, but the Prince wished to finish the bowl and when his host, really alarmed lest he quench his wits, refused to refill his glass, he gripped the bowl himself; Macdonald gripped the opposite side and, amid much laughter, they pulled the bowl in two! Needless to say, the pieces were treasured carefully and carefully mended. 'Prince Charlie's Bowl' was on show at the Highland Exhibition in Inverness for the last time in 1930, for, carelessly packed, it was hopelessly smashed on the return journey to its owner, a descendant of that Anne already mentioned.

Next day Flora Macdonald and Neil MacEachan left early to ride to Portree, leaving 'Kingsburgh' to bring the Prince by a footpath to the Royal Hotel (then a thatched inn) where Captain Donald Roy Macdonald was to meet them and guide the Prince to young 'Raasay' and his boat (see Chapter 5). But 'Kingsburgh' had no easy journey, for the Prince insisted on visiting one or two who had been wounded in his service, including Dr. Macleod, who lived with his daughter, Ann, in Eyre House, better known as 'Tot Miss Ann', on the hill above Snizort Manse. This house was long famous for its 'water ghost'. Flora must have been thankful indeed when she said farewell to Charles Edward at Portree and knew him safely *en route* for Raasay, her responsibility ended. Before leaving Kingsburgh he had given Mrs. Macdonald a lock of his hair which she shared with Flora, but the touching farewell so often said to have taken place at Portree between Prince Charles and Flora was described by an eye-witness as follows:

The Prince: I believe, Madam, I owe you a crown of borrowed money.
Flora: Only half a crown.

This he paid her, then saluted her and said: 'For all that has happened I hope, Madam, that we shall meet in St. James's yet.'

The sheets he had used at Kingsburgh were folded away to be shrouds, the one for Mrs. Macdonald, the other for Flora; his room was kept as he had left it until Dr. Johnson occupied it and lit the Prince's half-burnt candle!

Flora Macdonald was imprisoned for a time and then, after being something of a lion in London, where her detention was more nominal than real and included being presented to some of the royal dukes, she returned to Skye, travelling as Miss Robertson to avoid the fuss her own name produced everywhere. Later she married Allan Macdonald, 'Kingsburgh's' son and heir. They farmed Flodigarry until, in about 1760, Allan inherited Kingsburgh. Here they found that, as in other ages, farming did not pay and they, having lost in three years no less than 327 head of cattle and horses, decided to emigrate to America. This they did very shortly after Dr. Johnson's visit to them, sailing in 1774. In America Allan and two of his sons fought in the War of Independence, holding His Majesty's commissions in the Royal Highland Emigrant

Regiment; later Allan (then a Brigade Major) and one son
were captured. Flora also was made a prisoner and 'stood
in danger of her life'. They lost almost everything they
possessed. Later she and her daughter Fanny returned to
Skye (see Chapter 9), where her husband and sons soon
joined them. Her half-sister Annabella and her husband
now had a tack of Kingsburgh, so Allan and Flora went to
live in the tiny house of Peinduin , and here she died in
1790, bequeathing to her children as her two dearest possessions her lock of the Prince's hair and his silver shoe-
buckle. A window commemorating Flora Macdonald can
be seen in St. Columba's Church in Portree.   It is in the
west wall and its three lights depict the story of Esther
saving her people. The signature of her granddaughter
Fanny, cut with a diamond, is on one of the windows of the
present Adam house of Kingsburgh; tradition has it that
Fanny scratched it there the night before her wedding. In
the garden, roses planted by Flora still bloom.

In telling the story of the Prince we have gone too far
upon our road and must now return to Monkstadt and the
road which leads past the Kilmuir tweed centre into the
little town of Uig, with its lovely wooded glens and its
hospital. Said to have got its name from the Norse 'Ogr'
(Bay), Uig lies on a very beautiful one, and King Edward
VII himself opened the pier. Uig was well in the forefront
of the Land Reform agitation and was one of the places
visited by the Navy. Anxious to disperse the crowd which
naturally attended their landing, an officer of the Marines
inquired of one man near him why he was not at work.
'Who could possibly contemplate the restoration of dilapi-
dated footwear during a state of war?' was the reply. It is
not recorded that this officer made any further inquiries.

Witches are said to have been plentiful in Uig. As late

as 1881 an Elder of the Free Church there applied to a
J.P. for a warrant against a witch. Near here, too, lived the
old woman of whale fame. Three fishermen, so goes the
story, had as boys greatly annoyed and teased an old
woman. When, at last, they got a boat of their own, they
so constantly lost their nets and their catches that they
were on the brink of ruin. All this damage was caused by a
large whale who had taken up its abode in Loch Snizort.
The men made various attempts to get rid of it and at last
succeeded in driving a three-pronged pitchfork into its
side. Next day the old woman whom they had once annoyed
was found dying with three wounds in her side. The whale
was never seen again. Round about 1660 whale and seal
meat formed an important part of the island diet, which
makes this story a strange one though, of course, it may be
very much older; normally those animals whose form a
witch was liable to take, as for instance a cat or a hare,
were not eaten.

From Uig to Kingsburgh we travel by the oldest road in
Skye. In 1799 a government survey was made with the
object of turning one or more bridle-paths into roads and
so opening up the island, and this survey states that the
only highway 'is a good horse road from Uig to Kingsburgh'.

Not far from Uig, by the loch shore, lie the ruins of
Caistel Uisdean, a fortress built for himself by Hugh, next
of kin to Donald Gorm Mor, Lord of Duntulm. The fort had
neither windows nor doors, entrance being through the
roof only. Some such shelter Hugh certainly needed, since
he plotted ceaselessly against his by no means mild kins-
man (see Chapter 6).

The road to Cuidrach—the Place of the Forceful, or
Determined, One—takes off on the right a little farther

along the main road. Its name is said to refer to Do'all MacIain ic Shamus, who received Cuidrach from the then Macdonald as a reward for his prowess in battle (see Chapter 16).

The road to Portree crosses two biggish rivers, the Hinnisdal and the Romesdal, both once good trout streams. They are said to have got their names when early Norse settlers saw in them a resemblance to the original Hinnisdal and Romesdal rivers in Norway. Both run through beautiful country. Between them lies Kingsburgh in its woods down by the sea. There are various traditions as to the origin of the name: one claims that James V landed here when he visited Skye, and slept in the old house. Another holds that Kingsburgh means Cinnisboro, or Tax-town, and that it levied taxes on all who passed up or down Loch Snizort, then a highway. It is even claimed that Cuchullin himself was asked to pay tax here.

My father and I were at Kingsburgh at the time of King George V's long illness. About two miles away, up the hill, lived an old man of over eighty; he had been a stalker and had been one of those present when King George, as a boy, had shot his first stag. He was intensely anxious, as was the whole island, for news of the King. Every night, in the black dark—for it was a wet and cloudy winter—he walked down to us for news, and every night the news seemed less hopeful. Then came the great storm, one of the worst I have seen in the Hebrides: all night long the house shook and thunder growled. After breakfast my father and his setter Nora went out to look at the weather, and Nora was lifted off her feet and blown across the lawn: I never saw so frightened a dog. Throughout the day the storm raged and snow fell in heavy squally showers, but by evening the wind began to drop a little. Our usual visitor arrived. This time he did not ask 'How is my King?' but 'Is my King still alive?' We said that he was, but that there was still no change or improvement. 'He will do now', said the old man.

Next night, to our surprise, he did not come, but a slight improvement in the King's condition was reported. When the next day again passed without a visit we feared the walk through the storm had been too much for his heart, never very good, and went up to inquire and to bring him the latest (and good) news of his King. We found him busy on his croft and gave him the news. 'Ay, my King will do now', he said again. Then we asked why he had suddenly stopped his visits of inquiry and he replied quite simply: 'That was a Royal storm. It came for my King but he did not go with it. When a Royal storm is sent back empty, my mother told me, the one tor whom it came would live and do well. I never saw a Royal storm sent back before.' We asked him if he had ever seen a Royal storm before, and did they only come for the soul of a king? No, he said, any great man, and not every king, only the great. He himself had seen the one that came for Lord Kitchener, but Kitchener went with it. 'It is seldom that a Royal storm is sent back. But my King is a very great man.'

After Kingsburgh the road passes through the townships of Snizort and Kensaleyre. About a mile beyond Snizort, near the ruins of Reintra House, there is a waterfall on the Haultin river and in its pool dwells an Each Uisge, or water-horse. On the shore near Kensaleyre are two standing-stones, somewhat discoloured and spotted, as are the rocks round about them. Of them the following story is told.

These stones were originally placed there, in a long ago time, by the Fiennes, that they might stand their large cooking-pot upon them, in which deer were seethed whole and glorious venison stew made. But the time of the great stews departed, for all the deer vanished away from their usual haunts. The hunters hunted in vain, not even Bran could wind them. At last Caoilte, the swiftest and most silent among them, was sent alone to search. Fingal and the others gathered together hungrily to wait by the great pot. At last so hungry were they that they collected whelks and limpets from the rocks and filled the pot with them, stewing them in the milk of the Grey-cheeked Cow, a famous animal who grazed in Hinnesdal and whose bed was the Kid Rock (Creag nam Meann) behind Kingsburgh. Caoilte at length found the deer in a corrie in the Cuchullins and gave a shout which could be heard by the Fiennes on Loch Snizort shore, and they threw down the shell-fish stew, spattering the rocks with it, which have ever since been called Rocks of the Mouthful (Creagan a' Bhalguinn) and have remained spotted and discoloured.

At the head of the Loch the road forks, the right fork leading past Skirnish, with its duns, to the main Portree–Dunvegan road, the left fork reaching the same road nearer Portree. The latter is the main bus route.

8

Portree to Edinbane

(As if sung by St. Columba and his monks when
putting out to sea)

O Lord of the Heights, whose eye encircles
The land and the sea, and smiles through the thunder,
Smile on us too, as sail we outward
To far blue Isles, with tales of the Wonder.

.   .   .   .

Fair be our breeze, as bear we onward
Our Christ and our Cross, our song and our altar.

(From 'The Iona Rainbow' by Kenneth Macleod.)

THE road to the north branches off from the south road
close to Portree School. It leads to Skye's northern wings,
Trotternish, Waternish, and Duirinish, containing many of
her best views. Many people believe that it is from her
wings and her Gaelic name, Eilean Sgiathanach (Winged
Isle), that the name Skye comes. Ptolemy of Alexandria
(A.D. 200) refers to the island as Sketis, while the ancient
Celtic name 'Skeitos' has become Sgiath in modern Gaelic.
Adamnan knew it as Scia. This 'wing' derivation certainly
sounds very probable, more probable than the other version
which claims that 'Skye' is Scandinavian, derived from a
Norse word Ski (cloud). This school of thought takes its
stand on the fact that cloud or mist is what would first and
most forcibly attract the notice of any stranger visiting
the island, whereas to notice the 'wings' requires a map.
Obviously this school has never tried (as the early Scandinavian settlers most certainly did) to sail round the despised

wings. Of course, many place-names in Skye undoubtedly
are Scandinavian, but they date from a later time than
Ptolemy—four or five centuries later. A third suggestion,
once seriously put forward by certain Celtic antiquaries,
was that in Skye stood the temple, known to Greek fable,
of Apollo among the Hyperboreans, and that the Gaelic
name of the island refers to the wings of the Greek god!
The name may, in fact, even belong to some old forgotten
pre-Celtic tongue.

About four miles from Portree the road to Snizort and
Uig (in Trotternish) branches off. Close to this fork was the
gipsies' camp. Before the First World War its occupants
used to trek all over Europe—to Spain, Italy, the Balkans,
or the North—but always in the end the longing for the sea
mists would seize them and back to Skye they would come.
The camp became almost a township (until the authorities decided to move it in 1951) and though families
continued to come and go it always had some occupants.
The tents, made from tarpaulins stretched over hazel or
willow hoops, had stone foundations and stove-pipe
chimneys—and even wireless aerials and Tilley lamps.

Half a mile farther on the road passes the township of
Carbost and crosses the Snizort river, at one time the
boundary between the lands of Macdonald and Macleod.
Here in 1539 the Battle of Trouterness, probably the most
important in Skye's clan wars, was fought. The long series
of fights between Macleods and Macdonalds had for its
main aim the holding by the Macleods or the seizing by
the Macdonalds of the rich promontory of Trotternish. The
Macdonalds seized it, were driven out by an avenging
Macleod rally, then returned, seized it once more and, this
time determined to be on the safe side, drove out the Macleod
holders of the land at the spear's point. While so employed

they met a hastily gathered Macleod force on the banks of the Snizort and here on the moor the Battle of Trouterness (Trotternish) was fought and won. It was said that many Macleod heads were cut off, by order of Donald Gorm Macdonald, and flung into the water, and that these floated down and were caught in the yair at the mouth of the Snizort river, known ever since as Coirre-nan-Ceann, the 'Yair of the Heads'. After this victory the Macdonalds moved from Sleat to Duntulm the better to hold their spoils, and the King of Scotland, on being appealed to in the matter, accepted a *fait accompli* and granted Trotternish to them. Nevertheless, news of this battle confirmed him in his resolution to visit Skye in person the following summer.

Below the present bridge, between it and the sea, is a small islet round which the river forks, and which from pagan times until quite recently has been in use as a graveyard. The outline of a tiny church, about twenty-two feet long, can still be traced, and this is believed to have been built by St. Columba himself and to have been the first Christian church in Skye, though Monkstadt also claims that honour (see Chapter 7). Between the river and the road is the large boulder from which the saint used to preach. It was always St. Columba's practice to adapt pagan customs and beliefs to his own Christian teaching, and so it seems probable that because this little island burying-ground must have been a sacred place to the people whom he had come to convert, he chose it for his church.

That it was far too small to have been used as a burying-ground by even a small community for over 1,200 years does not seem to have troubled anyone, saint or pagan, at all. But that is a thing that never has troubled Skye, though it would seem more than time that the law or rule or custom which permits a new burial in any grave after an elastic fifteen years be altered. There is the story of a funeral in south Skye in 1949, when a skeleton was dug up in opening a 'new' grave. The skull rolled to the feet of one of the mourners, who lifted it, surveyed it critically, and remarked: 'Ay, that'll be Katie.' Which reminds me of the story of a Skye lady of olden days who had a tongue and did not suffer fools gladly. She had an acquaintance, an elderly spinster of the bore variety with very noticeable sticking-out teeth, who gushed. One day they met in Prince's Street; the old lady tried to pass by unseeing but the bore came up gushingly and exclaimed: 'I don't think you recognize me, Mrs. M.' 'My dear', replied the owner of the tongue, 'I would know your skull on the sea-shore.'

In later times St. Columba's little church was replaced by a larger and more elegant building, and from the road it is the ruins of this latter which can be seen today.

St. Columba's disciple and biographer, Adamnan, records how, before he reached Skye, the saint saw in a vision that he would be greeted on landing by an old man who would ask for baptism and, on receiving it, would die, and that this vision was fulfilled. Skye tradition goes farther and tells how, when St. Columba and his monks landed from their coracles on a beach near Snizort, they saw, somewhat to their dismay, an armed party approaching them. The monks pressed round their leader and lifted high the Cross. The warriors replied by opening their ranks so that the bearers of a rough skin litter might pass through. This litter the bearers set down before St. Columba and from it stepped a very old man, helped by a youth, his grandson. They approached the saint, and the young man explained that his grandfather was Artbrannan, chief of this part of Skye, and had heard much of Christianity and believed in the 'new God'. He had seen in a dream that he should not

die until Skye was visited by a holy man who would bap-
tize him. Since then, watch had been kept for the coracles
of the monks. He now came in search of baptism, for he was
very old and very tired. St. Columba spoke to the old chief
and baptized him, and as the holy water touched his forehead he fell dead at the saint's feet. The monks were rather
nervous of what effect this sudden death might have upon
the old chief's wild and well-armed followers, but apparently it was what they had been warned to expect. Lifting
the body back on to the litter, as on to a bier, they immediately formed themselves into a funeral procession and set
out for the little island in the Snizort river, the youth at
their head and the saint and his monks chanting as they
followed. Here the old chief was given Christian burial in
the presence of all his people, and over his grave they, with
the help of St. Columba and his monks, built the little
church.

In the time of the Napoleonic Wars the fear of 'Boney'
landing was not confined to England, and many Skye
families buried treasures for greater safety. There is a
tradition that once a French privateer was sighted and
much silver and plate was hurriedly buried in this old
graveyard. A big flood some fifty years later, which submerged the island, gave the story new life by washing up
a number of old silver spoons and forks and a few old
pieces of jewellery, but for obvious reasons no one has ever
searched for this hoard.

The new burial-ground is on the hill opposite, the hill
upon which a little white house called Caroline Hill once
stood. This house was a memorial to the American War of
Independence, for it is said to have been given its most un-
Skye-like name by an old Captain Macdonald who emigrated to Carolina with many other Skye Macdonalds,

lived most of his life there and fought in the War of Independence, after which event he returned to Skye, acquired the hill, and named it after the New World State he loved. The house is now a ruin. Its last occupant was old Miss Jessie Macleod of Gesto, who went there after her brother, Kenneth Macleod of Greshornish, died in 1869. She was the source of many of the old stories and facts in this book. My grandmother, her niece, used to drive over from Greshornish to see the old lady, as she then was, sometimes taking my mother with her. As a child I loved stories of that little house, with its drawing-room gay with spring flowers and almost fabulously valuable Indian embroideries and rugs and Kashmir shawls, and of old 'Aunt Jessie' herself with her stiff silk frock, soft lace cap, and young, bright eyes. The cap in particular was fascinating, for she began to wear one at the great age of twenty-seven when she went to keep house for her brother, as a sign that she had put away girlish things, youth, and frivolity, and was now the responsible mistress of a household, still prepared to be interested in the love affairs of her nieces, perhaps, but far too old to have any of her own!

When the visitors arrived, port wine and the thinnest of thin biscuits were served for the ladies, but ginger wine and little sweet cakes were produced for my mother and her sisters. Though she had so long ruled a tea-planter's household, Great-grand-aunt Jessie had *no* opinion of afternoon tea as a meal and certainly would not consider it seemly to serve it to her guests.

The road next passes by Skeabost Bridge post office and runs through the Skeabost woods between the once-famous mile of beech hedges. In the latter half of the nineteenth century, when Lachlan Macdonald built the present house of Skeabost, 'as rich as Skeabost' was a proverb in Skye;

now the once-lovely woods have outlived their allotted
span and have been cut, and the house has become an
hotel. It was on Skeabost that the Gaelic poetess Mhairi
Mhor nan Oran was born about 1821. She was among those
whose writings helped in Land Reform.

After Skeabost comes the township of Bernisdale and
then another belt of trees running down to the edge of the
little sea loch, Loch Treaslane, marks the site of what was
once Treaslane House. It was at one time the property of
one of the Martins of Marishadder, John Martin, founder of
the Uig Hospital, now the maternity hospital for Skye.

After Treaslane the road passes Tayinloan, in the days of
horses a busy inn but now a private house. It is always
worth slowing down here to look for unexpected flowers in
blossom on the bridge parapet, or in the woods where a
lovely wild garden is in process of formation. Soon after
Tayinloan comes the gate-lodge and woods of Lynedale.
Once these two were one property. The time to pass here is
in February, when the woods are a white carpet of snowdrops as far as the eye can reach. The bulbs here, as at
Gesto, Greshornish, and Orbost, were originally brought
back from the Crimea by Skye men who served in the
Crimean War, but they have thriven and spread like a
native plant.

Lynedale was once the property of that Alexander Macdonald who helped to build the Highland Railway and to
blast out of the solid rock that piece of line from Strome
Ferry to Kyle of Lochalsh which was proudly advertised as
the most expensive twelve miles of railway in the world;
but, for Skye, his chief title to fame is that he introduced
the first 'swing plough' in 1791, thereby revolutionizing
farming in the island. He it was who planted the Lynedale
woods. Tree-planting must have become a fashion in Skye

at about that time for the woods at Orbost, Greshornish, Dunvegan, and Gesto all date from that same period, but the great storm in the early 1920's swept away in one night all the wood at Orbost, about half that at Greshornish, and over 4,000 trees at Dunvegan. Dunvegan was an arresting sight the following summer with the giants tossed down dead all over the hill slopes and the ground between them solid blue with wild hyacinths, joyful in the unexpected sunlight.

Next comes the tiny township of Kildonan. Its name is all that remains of the old church of St. Donan, once the parish church of Snizort. Soon after this the road passes through Flashader, with its dun, its church, and its beautiful views of the Outer Islands, to Borve. Only one or two houses and its dun now remain. Of the latter the tale is told that it was a fairy fort inhabited by the Sithichean. The people of Borve found them a great bother and decided to drive them away, so one day they rushed about crying: 'The fort is on fire! The fairies' fort is on fire! They will all be burnt!' Out tumbled the fairies, the little old women crying: 'Dun Borbh is on fire, without dog or man! My little clews![1] My little bags of meal!', while the little men cried: 'Torr a Bhulg is on fire! My hammer and my anvil! Also my little bellows! Oh, my little bellows!' When they found it was a hoax they were so angry that they left the district, and the township never throve again.

After Borve the road runs down the south shore of Loch Greshornish to Edinbane. Loch Greshornish had its excitement in the Second World War. The people of Edinbane and Greshornish were wakened by a terrific noise of explosions echoing from hill to hill. A seaplane was dropping depth-charges into the loch in the hope of

[1] Balls of thread.

destroying a U-boat believed to have taken refuge there. From all accounts even the most super thunderstorm wasn't in it, and next day there was the further excitement of several mysterious and curious craft come a-hunting. But the Navy is very silent.

Loch Greshornish had its excitements in older days also. There was the summer of the sharks, when no one dared to bathe, and, stranger by far, there was the Whiskered Stranger. It had been a very hot summer and icebergs were known to have broken loose from the ice-floes and drifted into waters where usually they were unknown. One may have been his means of transport. So it was thought. Anyhow, one autumn evening an old man went fishing off the rocks at Dhubaig. This, as its name of Black Bay implies, is a rather eerie place, its Golden Cave being believed to be one of the entrances to the great cave at Harlosh—the one out of which the little dog came with all his hair singed off (see Chapter 15). Intent on his fishing, the old man heard nothing until something disturbed him and he glanced up, to find (so he maintained) the Devil himself looking at him over the top of a nearby rock. This apparition was completely black, with very long whiskers and ghastly, gloating eyes. When it opened its mouth to speak the unfortunate fisherman saw the most terrible tusks. He turned, flung down his catch, and fled. Straight to the Manse he ran (three or four miles over heather) and there and then signed the pledge. Next day some bold spirits went out well armed to search for the Devil, for the old man stuck to it that he *had* seen it and it *had* eaten his fish. They returned proudly displaying a full-grown walrus, the only one ever known to have visited Skye.

As soon as the road passes Edinbane it begins to climb and from its lower slopes there is an excellent view of the

township. It looks exactly like a chess-board or one of
those little wooden towns children get in boxes at Christmas and arrange in formal order on the carpet. Not real at
all. For Edinbane, unlike the other townships of Skye, did
not just grow: it was planned. It was planned by Kenneth
Macleod of Greshornish, Coinneach Mor Ghesto as he was
called, who not only laid out the crofts but took very
considerable trouble to ensure that among those he settled
there there should be one skilled craftsman for each necessary craft; mason, carpenter, smith, and so forth. The
result was a self-sufficing township, and one where sons,
taught by skilled fathers, kept up a high standard in the
various trades.

Kenneth Macleod was 'the Landlord' in Alexander
Smith's *A Summer in Skye*. He says of him: 'The Landlord
when he entered on the direction of his property exploded
every ancient form of usage.' Then follows a most interesting account of his schemes for his people and his methods:
his school, his 'penal settlement', his 'work for all' who
needed it, his emigration ship to Canada, which had orders
to remain there for some weeks so that it might bring back
to Skye any who changed their minds or became homesick;
above all, his hospital, which he founded in Edinbane—the
first in the island—and endowed sufficiently to support a
good doctor. In many of his schemes he was before his time.

The hospital and its doctors were a nine-days' wonder in
Skye in the early days and a source of many stories. There
is the tale of the young doctor who, newly appointed,
arrived with his wife to find a patient had just died in the
hospital. Horrified by the bad name this might give both
the hospital and himself, he and his wife placed the
corpse upright between them in his dog-cart, and drove
him home in this position so that all might see he had

left the hospital safe and well. This doctor's sojourn in
Skye was short.

Later there was a doctor who loved cleanliness and
taught that to wear a suit, unwashed, for more than a week
was both dirty and unhealthy. He himself always wore
light-coloured Shetland tweed suits which his housekeeper
washed regularly every Monday and hung out on the line,
to the joy of Edinbane's youth, who christened him 'Baggy
Knees'. He it was, too, who, being much troubled by bees
swarming in the hospital roof and alarming both patients
and staff, chloroformed them. The treatment was most
successful and soon the ground was thickly carpeted with
fallen bees. Everyone was delighted and went cheerfully
back to work; so, as soon as the anaesthetic wore off, did
the bees. Once when he was expecting friends his housekeeper decided to make a pigeon pie, but the pigeons would
not be caught. So she appealed to the doctor. He mixed
oatmeal and whisky and spread a feast for the birds. They
came, but so did the ducks, and their later efforts, when
very drunk, to waddle back to the burn were said to be a
sight worth seeing. The pigeons were duly caught and
made into a pie but alas! for all the good whisky wasted:
the pie tasted so strongly of the spirit that not even the
most polite guest could make shift to eat it.

9

Edinbane to Fairy Bridge

———————◆■◆———————

How beautiful they are, the lordly ones
Who dwell in the hills, in the hollow hills.

(From 'The Faery Song' in *The*
Immortal Hour by Fiona Macleod)

ABOUT a mile beyond Edinbane the road to Greshornish takes off to the right and the house chimneys can be seen in the distance amongst its trees. This was the home of Kenneth Macleod, who stands out of the shadows as the biggest figure of his generation (1809 to 1869) in the island. He was the last in the main line of the Macleods of Gesto, one of the oldest families in Skye, who could trace their descent back unbroken to Harold the Black, King (or Jarl) of Iceland, and from him, though in less well-proven fashion, to the great god Odin himself.

Kenneth Macleod's own life was as full of incident as a penny dreadful. As a young man, bereft of his inheritance, he left Skye to seek his fortune in India. There he was able to do a service for the Rajah of Hutival and in return received a grant of land in full possession and, what was perhaps even more important, they became lifelong friends. Wise planting of tea and indigo did the rest. He returned to Skye, still a comparatively young man, but wealthy beyond his neighbours' dreams, and tried to buy back Gesto, his ambition and the mainspring of most of his actions. But the then owner, the Macleod of Macleod of that day, would not sell. One does not lightly part with Naboth's vineyard. And so Kenneth Macleod bought Greshornish, Orbost, and Skeabost instead, the two former having once been connected with Gesto.

He got engaged to a very lovely girl, rather younger than himself, with whom he was deeply in love. She went to London with her parents to choose her trousseau, and disappeared. In vain her parents searched. They had no clue, so it was said. Kenneth rushed to London to search high and low for many months, both there and in Paris, then returned to Skye in such a mood that no one dared question him or condole, then or later. What really happened was never known, but the person most likely to know, his favourite sister Jessie, who kept house for him at Greshornish, most certainly believed he had found his bride in Paris, dying, and did the only thing left in his power, which was to see that she was well and lovingly cared for for the few weeks that remained. But the how and why of it 'Miss Jessie' either never knew or never told.

Like most Skye men, 'Greshornish' saw service. In the Indian Mutiny he raised a force of tenants on his Indian estates and commanded them in person. Later, when riding from Edinburgh to London, he was attacked by highwaymen and it is on record that the highwaymen concerned much regretted the encounter, as did a certain somewhat peppery member of the Parish Council who, annoyed at a meeting failing to accept his viewpoint, challenged Kenneth to a duel. 'Certainly', replied 'Greshornish', 'but I choose fists.' The duel did not come off.

His life was full of colour: the life of the East, with its sunshine and silks and jewels, was as real to him as the grey mists and homespun of Skye, and certainly to my childish ears tales of him were as of some legendary figure.

Even his servants were not ordinary. One was from India, a 'black man'. Who else ever had a cook who made herself mad fighting drunk on 'green tea' meant to be blended in the proportion of one teaspoonful to a pound but brewed by her on the stove, undiluted? This same cook, when over forty years old, had all her teeth out and promptly grew a third lot. The horrified travelling dentist· immediately removed these also.

Greshornish itself is a typical Skye 'manor' house. Low and white, well guarded from storms by a belt of thick trees, its front door is always open, as is the hospitable tradition of the island, where 'as mean as the key' became a proverb, and the views from its windows are unsurpassed. It is also properly furnished with a haunted room and a ghost. The ghost is reputed to be a man in a kilt, but no one now living appears to have seen him. In the haunted room, 'something' pulls off the bedclothes at midnight and the unfortunate occupant awakes shivering. In my childhood I met three people to whom this had happened in that room and who were convinced of the truth of the belief. But personally I have always slept there peacefully and my bedclothes have stayed on.

This was 'Miss Jessie's' room, where most of these stories were originally told. In those days it was furnished with a big four-poster bed. My mother, as a small girl, was a pet of her grand-aunt's and used to be asked on visits when, instead of being merely one of a nursery full at home, she suddenly became A Guest and A Very Important Person, so she loved it. She slept with her grand-aunt and the great joy was to keep awake, somehow, watching the firelight on the ceiling till 'Aunt Jessie' came to bed. Then she would be sorry for the poor little girl who couldn't go to sleep, would give her some of her own nightcap of gruel with

butter (!) in it, and could be coaxed into telling tales of
'When I was a little girl' or old Skye stories. Stories of how
'Aunt Jessie's' grandmother had danced at that last gay
ball at Duntulm, given to celebrate the birth of the heir.
Of how, when the oldest tenant came in to propose his
health, the music stopped, the guests gathered close,
glasses were raised in readiness as the old man raised his to
the baby, who had been carried in and was being proudly
held by his nurse. Then, in the waiting silence, the first
words of a Gaelic toast were heard, broken by a cry as the
old man fell forward unconscious, the undrunk toast spilt
upon the floor. 'Just a faint: too much excitement', said
the doctor. But, 'What did he see?' 'What an omen!',
whispered the guests. The fun grew fast and furious. The
ball was voted one of the best ever held. In' a matter of
months the baby boy fell from a window to his death; in
a matter of years Duntulm was a deserted ruin.

There were tales, too, of a Skye man whose name I cannot remember. Bold, careless, and quick of wit, he was always in trouble. One day he killed a man in a quarrel and
as the man had powerful friends and the duel, if it was one,
no witnesses, trouble seemed imminent. But the rogue was
too clever for them. He learnt where King James was
hunting and took care to be in his path. At sight of the
King he fell on his knees near the King's horse, giving all
the appearance of one who is slightly simple, and cried out:
'Pardon, my Lord King, pardon upon me.' 'Pardon you
for what?' asked the king. 'I knocked a man's hat off,
Sire.' 'You have our pardon', replied the King seriously,
'but why ask pardon for so small a crime?' 'Because the
man's head was in it, Sire', replied the rogue composedly.
The King, entertained by his wit, said that his pardon
stood. But later, for other misdeeds, he was banished

'never again to set foot on Scottish soil upon pain of death'. That sounded final, but after a few months in France he returned, was arrested and was to be executed. Again he appealed to King James, this time on the grounds that he had *not* set foot on Scottish soil; both his boots had an interlining of French earth. He eventually died in Skye most peacefully of old age.

There were stories, too, of Dr. Johnson, whose manners (or want of them) had left a lasting impression in the island (see Chapter 19). Also of Flora Macdonald and how she looked and spoke, what she said to the Prince and what he said to her (see Chapter 7). Though Grand-Aunt Jessie had never known Flora herself (she was born nine years too late) she had heard from her mother how indignant Flora Macdonald was when, after being taken as a prisoner to London, she became something of a 'lion' there (or should it be lioness?), but despite her best endeavours could never convince her admirers that her sympathies were *not* Jacobite and never had been, or that politics lacked interest for her. Yet in truth her family were mildly (admittedly *very* mildly) Hanoverian supporters, though of course Lady Clanranald, under whose care she had spent several years, was a zealous Jacobite. There were tales, too, of the attack by a French ship upon the one in which Flora and her daughter were returning from A ierica, of how she herself was wounded and how she encouraged the sailors by her fearlessness, even loading a gun herself when the gunner was hit, and how useful her first aid was, too, for, as 'Miss Jessie' did not hesitate to impress on her small grandniece, every mistress of a household must be something of a doctor. Certainly that was true in the Hebrides of her day.

Legend has turned Flora Macdonald into a rather

dreamy, romantic hero-worshipper, but the Flora Macdonald of real life was both practical and full of common
sense. Political views did not count when a man's life was
at stake, so she helped the Prince. Later she became an
inspiring and capable wife and mother, a most efficient
home-maker. When an over-gushing admirer praised her
courage, her resolution, her quick wit, she replied somewhat tartly that it was true she had imperilled her life for
both the House of Stuart and the House of Hanover but
she never saw that she was any the better for it.

Miss Jessie herself held Jacobite sympathies, though by
now such ideas were little more than fragrant dreams.
Traditional dreams, perhaps, and she would have been the
first to be horrified at any hint of disloyalty to the Queen.
She knew many stories of the Prince, his puppy-like clumsiness in women's clothes and his unforgettable, unassail-
able charm. But these were counterbalanced by stories of
gallantry of another sort. For example, the story of how
another plot was formed and a list (how foolish!) was made
of the names of those prepared to support yet a third
'Rising'. Secret agents got a copy: a copy that might
mean death to hundreds. They brought it to one of the
King's ministers. The '45 was not yet forgotten and an
agitated, though secret, buzz arose in Whitehall. A minister
brought the list to King George. 'Leave it with me', said
the King. 'But, Sire', pressed the minister, anxiously,
'preparations must be made. We have no other copy.
There is no time. . . .' The King looked at the door and the
minister left by it. The King looked at the list. The first
name on it was that of the Important Person from whom it
had been stolen. The King rang a bell. A secretary hurried.
Lord —— to wait upon His Majesty at once. Lord ——
entered. King George was seated by the fire toasting his

toes. 'A poor figure compared to the gallant and handsome young Prince' may have been in his lordship's mind. But the King picked up a paper—the list—opened it, held it out. 'Is this your property, my lord?' One glance at it and a stunned silence. 'Well, is it?' somewhat testily. What use to deny his own signature, his own handwriting? 'Yes, Sire.' 'Then hadn't you better burn it? It is abominably careless to leave such things about', and His Majesty, a king indeed, made room by the fire. That story, too, was told in the old four-poster bed.

Greshornish had its fairies also—down on the Aird where the greenest grass grew. At least, some said it was the fairies. When Kenneth Macleod first bought Greshornish he was surprised and puzzled to find that no sheep ever grazed on the Aird. He suggested to his shepherds that this good grazing should be used, but was always met with some excuse. At last he tackled the matter seriously and, after many attempts to evade the issue, a young shepherd told him that the Aird belonged to the fairies and they didn't like sheep there. If sheep grazed there the fairies would bewitch them and they would run round in circles till they died. A certain old shepherd had told him so. So to the old shepherd went 'Greshornish'. 'Sheep put on the Aird', said the old man, '*always* ran round in circles till they died.' Some did it sooner, some later, but they all did it. As a young man he had not believed it was the fairies, though he was told so; he had thought it was a special plant which grew there and nowhere else round about. He had gathered some of the leaves and taken them to the Muir of Ord market and shown them to other shepherds and drovers there. Two men from Ross-shire told him that the plant grew on their best pasture land and never harmed the sheep, but another man told him that it had killed his sheep in the same strange way. At this point, said the old shepherd, a man who had been listening joined in. He told them that everyone 'in the West' knew this was the fairies' plant but that he himself believed that where it grew plentifully the fairies were content that the sheep should share and then they throve on it, but when it was scarce the fairies bewitched any animal that touched it. 'So,' said the old man, 'I have never put sheep on the Aird again for, fairies or no fairies, sheep die there.'

Kenneth Macleod did not believe in fairies but he did believe in poisonous plants, so a box of the rare weed went to Edinburgh for information. Back came the reply. The plant was well known and not known to be poisonous. To be on the safe side, however, various tests had been made, also certain animals fed on it. The tests for poison were negative and the animals throve. Sheep could safely be grazed on it. So to the Aird the sheep went back. And in due course they ran round in circles till they died.

This time one of the dead sheep was sent to Edinburgh with an account of its death. The reply was: 'No sign of poison; the sheep was fat and had died of heart failure, probably caused by running so much.' Why it ran, who could say? 'Fairies', replied the shepherds with one voice. The Aird was left sheepless.

Some years passed and a botanist came to Greshornish. Interested in the story, he went out with a magnifying glass and studied the vegetation. He came in triumphant. On the plant in question were hundreds of tiny snails. No doubt they were poisonous and might not live in every district or climb at every season. So snails and more leaves went to Edinburgh for new tests. Once more came the reply: 'Snails and leaves harmless.'

'Greshornish' decided to try sheep on the Aird again and

this time to watch himself for the fairies. And watch he did, with his shepherds. The sheep throve and grew fat. The fairies, it seemed, had left the district, and, after a few weeks, watching ceased. Then one day came a shepherd. He had the same story to tell. He had found a dead sheep on the Aird and seen others running in circles. Kenneth Macleod hurried to the pasture. There were three sheep running round and round in circles—no man, no dog, no fox to scare them. A lovely, still evening and fat, healthy sheep running round and round till they died. 'Bewitched' seemed the only possible answer.

Next morning 'Greshornish' set off for Edinburgh with two dead sheep and a hamper of various greens. He found 'Edinburgh' much interested, but no sign of poison in sheep or vegetation. Then a microscope was produced and the animals studied under it. And there was the answer. In the mouth of each tiny snail shell was a yet more tiny insect, invisible to the naked eye. These appeared to come loose from their snail hosts at certain seasons and were then breathed in by the sheep, whose brains they ultimately reached, producing madness. On the brains of the two dead sheep clusters of the insects were found. Various means of dealing with the pest were devised and now on Aird of Greshornish no sheep run in circles but only graze in peace.

After the Greshornish turning, the main road mounts steadily and much more steeply than appears to the eye, as the moor on either side rises steadily and evenly also. Most motorists new to this hill are puzzled by their cars' sudden loss of power. Stron-an-ain is a good solid climb, its top is the highest point reached by any road in Skye. Up, up, up, and down, down, down, till the cross-roads at Fairy Bridge are reached. The right-hand fork goes to Waternish, the left to Dunvegan and Glendale and also back to Portree by Bracadale and Sligachan.

Fairy Bridge, itself a pleasant spot, with a brown peat burn spanned by a good stone bridge, a small grass triangle, and lovely views of hill and valley and the Eagles' Rock, has an evil reputation. It is strange how often cross-roads have. Though why, in this case, is in dispute. But before the preachings were held there only a very bold man would pass that way alone after dark and no horse would pass quietly, day or night. Some said it was fairy ground and that horses could see the fairies dancing on the green grass triangle. Others said a murder (some said three for good measure) had been committed there and that the ghost (or ghosts) of the victim might be seen. Certainly two men, at different times, were found dead there, and what had *they* seen ?

My grandfather, John Robertson of Orbost, was much puzzled by the shying of every horse at the bridge, whether driven, ridden, or led across. He himself, an experienced horseman and no believer in either ghosts or fairies, had just the same trouble with his horses as did those who feared the place. He believed that a rider or driver, himself nervous at the bridge, would convey his fear to his horse, causing it to shy, and that the beast did not forget and would always afterwards shy at its own remembered panic. One day he bought a new horse from Ireland. It came by sea to Dunvegan and so had not to cross Fairy Bridge. At that time, too, he had a friend from the south staying with him who had never before been in Skye and knew neither Skye geography nor Skye stories. This friend offered to try the new horse and my grandfather, seeing the chance of testing his theory, gave him directions for a ride which involved crossing Fairy Bridge twice. When the rider returned he was eagerly questioned about the horse. A good beast, he pronounced her, good tempered, steady and pleasant to ride, but evidently nervous of water as she had shied twice, both times while crossing a bridge. Curiously, too, it was the same bridge both times and she took no notice of the others they had crossed. Needless to add, it was Fairy Bridge.

At the time of the Disruption a noted Free Church preacher, the Rev. Roderick Macleod, held large prayer-meetings at Fairy Bridge, and it was after this that fear of the place began to die out. A little later no one objected to it for Land Reform meetings, for which it was a convenient centre.

And how are the mighty fallen! Fairy Bridge is now a bus-stop.

10

Waternish

———————◆●◆———————

St. Brendan and his monks on their voyages came
to an island, where was an old man.

*And the old man said to them, 'O holy men of God,
make haste to flee from this island. For there is a sea-
cat here, of old time, that hath grown huge through eat-
ing excessively of fish.' Thereupon they turned back
in haste to their ship. But lo, behind them they saw
that beast swimming through the sea, and it had great
eyes like vessels of glass.*

(From *Beasts and Saints*, by Helen Waddell)

IN spite of views noted for their beauty, even in this island
of beautiful views, and in spite of such modern improvements as a bus service, Waternish has always been curiously
forbidding. Every legend or historic tale about this peninsula is full of horror and gloom. Why, no one knows. Was it
perhaps the last hold of heathendom in Skye, as it certainly was of wolves? Whatever the reason, that feeling of
gloom persists. Even today Waternish contains a sect of
its own, more strictly imbued with the harsher doctrines
of Calvinism and more disapproving of the lighter side of
life than any other in the Island.

The Waternish road turns off to the north at Fairy Bridge,
whence it runs along the valley of the Bay river. On the
left of the road, though at some little distance from it,
where the river cleaves its way through a gorge to the sea,
stands the mound which is all that now remains of the

'Temple of Anaitis' (so called). What form of prehistoric building it was or of what period is not known. But Dr. Johnson visited Waternish to see it in 1773 and it was a mystery then as now. Its old Gaelic name is said to have been 'Teampuill-na-Annait' and so to have given rise to the Anaitis legend. This name of Annait or Annat is found all over Scotland. It has been interpreted as meaning the 'Water-place' from Celtic 'An' = water, because many are near water. Others suggest 'Ann' = a circle (Celtic) and claim that most Annats are near standing-stones (see Chapter 19). The most-favoured derivation seems to be from Ann, the Irish Mother of the Gods, and those who hold this view claim that the Annats are always near a revered spot, where either a mother-church or the cell of a patron saint once stood. Probably Annat does, in fact, come from an older, pre-Celtic tongue, and belongs to an older people whose ancient worship it may well commemorate. The curious shape of the Waternish Temple of Anaitis and its survival make it seem likely that it was something of importance in its day, built with more than usual care and skill. Perhaps the Temple tradition is correct—but whose, if so, and to what gods? One cannot help wondering if cats played any part in its ritual, and if so, if any faint memory remains, for the nickname of the people of this wing was 'Na Caits' = The Cats, and not far off, by one of the tributary burns on the right of the roadway, there stands a small cairn, crowned by a long, sharp stone somewhat resembling a huge claw. This is the 'Cats' Cairn'.

Two hundred years ago a Dunvegan boy aged twelve was sent by his parents to carry a message to his grandmother who lived in Waternish. This was something of a treat and the boy set off gladly. On his return journey, however, a thunderstorm broke out and the lad took refuge in an empty, half-ruined cottage near the road-side. It was dusk, and tired by his long walk he fell asleep, to be wakened some hours later by a curious scrabbling sound. He opened his eyes and there, near where he lay, was a huge black cat. It was not watching him, however, but gazing unblinkingly up through the hole in the roof that used to serve as a chimney. Through this hole were descending two more cats. As soon as all three reached the ground they changed before the boy's astonished eyes into three old women, two of whom he knew well as they lived near his parents in Dunvegan. That they were witches he had no doubt. The three soon saw him and came over to peer curiously at him. 'He's asleep', said one. 'He *may* be', said number two more cautiously. 'It does not matter whether he is asleep or not', said the third and biggest cat-woman decidedly. 'If he is asleep he knows nothing and if he is awake he will not dare to say anything.' 'For if you do', she added, looking at the frightened lad who was desperately shamming sleep, 'we will hear it and we will see it: we will find you and we will kill you. I put the Fear upon you.' She made a sign with her hand and all three, resuming their cat form, scrambled back through the chimney-hole and the boy was alone.

The storm had ended and the boy lost no time in returning home, where his absence had caused no anxiety as he was thought to be with his grandmother. But he seemed utterly exhausted, could not eat, could not sleep, and would not leave the house. The old black cat had overdone it and his fear showed so plainly that his mother at last persuaded him to tell her the cause. He told her all and named two of the witches. His mother hurried to the minister, but he was away, and the woman, anxious for advice, confided in a neighbour. Soon all the village knew, under an oath of secrecy. So did the witches. But nothing happened. For a year nothing happened. The boy, his secret told, regained his health and forgot, as boys do, and the following summer his mother again sent him with a message to Waternish. Again he was caught by a storm and again took shelter in the little ruin. Next day his body was found where the cairn now stands. He appeared to have been done to death by long, sharp claws.

The road runs on, above it on the right a heather-covered hillside, below it to the left a wonderful vista of sea and cliffs, with the Outer Isles blue in the distance. A view worth coming far to see. All round about, in every suitable corner, globe flowers bloom in their season. These, in a tradition undoubtedly Scandinavian, are no common flower but a sign that in deep caverns beneath their roots the mountain gnomes (trolls?) are smelting gold, and the fumes of the precious metal rise in the form of these golden balls. It is interesting to note that as well as these subterranean smiths, the smiths and armourer of Clan Macleod lived and worked near Stein.

Below the road, at the river mouth, sheltered by steep cliffs, nestles the little township of Bay with its four crofts, whose owners cultivate this rich though tiny delta.

The backbone of the peninsula is Dunhalin. At its base there are still faint traces of ancient wolf-traps to be seen. Indeed, so comparatively recent are they that tradition still lingers of how a hunter accidentally fell into his trap and was saved by his companion, one Gille Chriosd Chaim, who caught the wolf by the tail and so held it.

The road passes from view to view until a lane to the left leads us down to the village of Stein on the seashore. Stein was deliberately built as a fishing village in an attempt to start fishing as an organized industry in Skye. But organized industries do not flourish in the Western Isles and Stein is once more a free crofting township, though it still has its boats and an interest in them. Its name, Stein, is said to be Norse and to go back to the days when some of King Haco's ships sought shelter there. The first road ever made in Skye (as opposed to a 'horse track') ran from Kylerhea to the then new and important village of Stein. The first survey for this road began in 1799 and it is now the main road by Broadford and Bracadale to Dunvegan and Stein.

Above Stein lies Waternish House and farm. Old Captain Macdonald of Waternish is still remembered for his unusual power over animals. Perhaps his most amazing feat was taming a pair of wild golden eagles so that when out on the hill, if he shot a rabbit and held it up they would swoop down and take it from his hand. A tame seal left the sea at his whistle and flopped after him like a clumsy dog, and on his lawn lived in peace together the weirdest collection of creatures; an otter played with some retired otter-hounds and terriers; a white hare, some rabbits, and a fox ignored one another politely, for the lawn was sanctuary and the sanctuary laws were firmly enforced by a tame deer who had lost one eye. She could still see to use her hoofs, as the terriers well knew. Captain Macdonald had served in the Crimean War and was one of those who brought back snowdrops to Skye. I still remember his intense scorn of 'this new effeminate afternoon tea'. His nephew and successor at Waternish, the late Mr. Allan Macdonald, was reputed to be the only man then living who really knew and understood the Macdonald genealogy and clan history.

Passing Waternish House, the road goes on to Ardmore Bay and township, another road taking off to the right to the townships of Geary, Knockbreck, and Gillen. Ardmore nearly had the honour of sheltering Prince Charles Edward, for the boat bringing the Prince and Flora Macdonald to Kingsburgh ran, after eight hours battling with the storm, close to Ardmore Point hoping to land there, but was fired on by soldiers stationed on the headland and so passed on.

Near Ardmore is Crec a Chrochaidh or the 'Hanging Hill', where the son of Judge Morrison of Lewis was hanged on a gibbet made from his own oars because he had received hospitality at Dunvegan and, after accepting it, landed on Isle Isay and killed three Macleods. Before his execution he asked time to pray, which was granted him. Many years later a number of silver coins were found hidden in a crevice of the rock on which he knelt. It is supposed that he utilized his last moments in hiding them to disappoint his executioners.

Above Ardmore are the ruins of Trumpan Church with its curious old basalt font or holy-water stoup, said to be never dry, however often emptied or however warm the weather. In the churchyard is an interesting old carved tombstone and the 'Heaven Stone'. This is a monolith with a small round hole in it. It was long believed that should anyone, led up to the stone with their eyes shut and so blinded, succeed in putting a finger through the hole at the first attempt, that person was certain to attain Heaven. He who failed in this test had another destination. The old church was once the centre of life and interest in the peninsula. In its graveyard lie the bones of that ill-starred Lady Grange, though indeed, if the gossip concerning her was true, hers was a case of 'character is fate'. Still, there can have been few more unhappy lives than hers and few stranger.

Lady Grange was the daughter of John Cheesly of Dalry, that man of most violent temper who murdered President Lockhart. She was married (some say against her will, others say so that she might spy upon him) to James Erskine, Lord Grange. She had inherited her father's almost insane temper and there were frequent quarrels. Lord Grange, with Lord Lovat and others, was engaged in plans for the return of the Stuarts, as she discovered. The story goes that she concealed herself beneath a daybed in the room in which they met, then sprang out and denounced their 'treacherous plot', threatening to disclose it to the Government. However that may be, it seems certain that she knew of their plot and that her husband either believed or pretended to believe that she was a great danger to its success and must be removed. He persuaded his friends of the necessity and after a struggle so furious that the unfortunate woman lost two of her teeth she was abducted, some say by order of Lord Lovat, others again by order of Macleod of Dunvegan and Macdonald of Sleat, and carried to Skye, where she was concealed, first in a hut on the Macleod estates and then on Macdonald land in Uist. Meanwhile her husband gave out that she was very ill of a fever; next day she 'died' of it and was 'buried' with a large and much-advertised funeral. But rumours of her abduction got about, as rumours will, and to make all safe she was removed to St. Kilda, where she lived a most miserable life for many years. No one in the island could speak English, Lady Grange could speak no Gaelic and apparently never tried to learn it. Whatever her temper, she was cultured and accustomed to a highly civilized and intellectual way of life. She was imprisoned in the most primitive community in Britain, unable to speak to her guardians and without occupation, suffering their privations (she had only a 'crusie' for light, for instance) but without their interests. When at length she was brought back to Skye, many years later, it was said no one could have recognized her. But her spirit remained unbroken. She was now imprisoned in a cottar's house in Waternish, but here she was better treated and happier, she was allowed clothes and some better food, and the woman of the house was kind to her and taught her to spin. Lady Grange spun eagerly and sent her wool with that of her neighbours to Inverness wool market. Inside one of the hanks, however, was a letter to her friends, written in blood as she had neither ink nor pencil. The purchaser of the wool found and forwarded the letter and her friends, much concerned, approached the Government on her behalf. A ship to search for her was promised, but all this was in the disturbed years before the '45 when there were many wheels within wheels in politics, so Lord Grange was able to stop the ship sailing. Her friends then subscribed, fitted out a ship, and sent it to Skye. But Macleod had word of its coming, Lady Grange was removed by boat to a cave—still known as Lady Grange's Cave—in the south-west cliffs near Macleod's Maidens. From this cave she was eventually taken to Uist once more. It is said that beside her in the boat lay a noose of rope attached to a great stone and that the boatman had orders, should a ship approach, to throw her overboard and make very sure she sank quickly. This danger, too, she survived, and returned to Waternish, to die there just before the '45. A great funeral for 'the poor strange lady who came ashore and died' was held to Duirinish churchyard and, according to McCullough, cost Macleod of Dunvegan £30. 15s. 5d., a large amount at that time. But, says tradition, in that coffin were but stones and turf, the lady herself being buried secretly in Trumpan churchyard. So ended fifteen years of misery.

Trumpan Church was a ruin, however, before that secret burial, for one quiet Sunday, when all but a few old people and children were at church, the Macdonald galleys sailed silently into the bay: silently they were beached, silently the Macdonalds left them and approached the church. It was soon surrounded and set on fire as a revenge for the Massacre of Eigg. Being a thatched building it burned readily, and when the congregation, rendered desperate by the flames, attempted to escape they were put to the sword. One woman did escape, badly wounded, but able to send a child for help. The sentry on the Castle tower saw the flames and he also gave warning. The Macleods came with what strength they could muster close at hand. The Macdonalds had been delayed by a force of old people and boys whose strength they could not estimate. By the time they reached the shore the tide had gone down and their galleys lay high and dry, while hidden from them the Macleod forces, which had crossed the loch, were already landing. A terrible battle ensued, in which it is said that the Macleods, much outnumbered, had recourse to waving the Fairy Flag, though others say that it was not then, but at the third battle of Waternish, that the Flag was waved and that the Macdonalds immediately saw a great host approaching (which, in fact, was not of this world) and fled. Be that as it may, the Macleods were victorious, the Macdonalds being almost annihilated. The dead, too many to bury, were laid, friend and foe together, beneath a dyke, and it and the wall which topped it pushed down upon them. So, ever since, it has been known as Blar Milleadh Garaidh—the Battle of the Spoiling of the Dyke—and it is said that those tilling the fields still find human bones.

Today in many a clachan in the Isle of Mists and rain
They tell at winter ceilidh this story o'er again;
And many a timid cailleach, when the evening shadows
* fall,*
Avoids the place that bears the name 'Destruction of the
* Wall'.*

(From 'The Burning of Trumpan Church', by **F. T.**
Macleod, in *The Songs of Skye*)

11

Fairy Bridge to Dunvegan

————◦■◦————

Dr. Johnson to the Lady of Macleod:

Keep to the rock; it is the very jewel of the Estate. It looks as if it had been let down from Heaven by the four corners, to be the residence of a Chief.

THIS is a road of birds. Hawks of various kinds, merlins and buzzards, kestrels, sparrow-hawks, hen-harriers, and peregrine falcons do sentry-go on the telegraph posts, so sure of their lordship over mountain and valley that they do not move for the passing car. On the wires gather the little birds—migrants in their thousands at some seasons.

In the olden days when the paddle-steamer *Glencoe* (formerly the *Mary Jane*, who sank and was raised again) moved slowly but comfortably from Mallaig to Portree, pausing at each pier to have her engines reversed by hand with crowbars, travellers to Dunvegan were late upon their way. A twenty-three-mile drive, with the younger members of the party walking up the hills to rest the horses, does not make for speed either and so it was not unusual to be on the road until midnight or long after; and that is the time for seeing things, especially in the winter—such things as the Aurora Borealis in every colour, rose-pink, red, green, or rainbow coloured; and lunar rainbows, those fairly common but seldom seen pure white moon-bows. Last year we saw a still stranger thing, though at an earlier hour. The sun had set but it was not yet dark and the opal glow of the moonrise was beginning to fan out from behind a hill, when we noticed a complete, scintillating green rainbow which contained no trace of any other colour at all. It began pale, soft, and slightly misty, became clear, sharp, and vivid, and in a few moments faded out. A quite perfect bow. Rainbows of the ordinary variety are very common in Skye; even complete double bows are not uncommon. Once, over Loch Bracadale, a perfect triple bow appeared. Perhaps in Skye we need extra strong assurance that the Deluge really is over!

In due course the road reaches another fork: to the right lies Dunvegan, straight on leads to Roag, Harlosh, and Bracadale, also (ultimately) Portree again. The road to the right runs swiftly down to the sea at Loch Dunvegan, once Loch Follart or Fallart, where the second largest township in the island shelters below the castle woods. Dunvegan might almost be termed a 'model village'. It has everything a little town should have, including a piped water-supply, two churches, a village hall (and a most excellent one), and an outstanding modern secondary school built just before the Second World War. In this last they claim to have been lucky, for it might so easily have been someone other than the Director of Education in person who fell through the floor of the old school.

On the right of the road before it reaches the sea lie two graveyards, the new and the old. This latter, with the ruined church of Kilmuir within its walls, contains the graves of the MacCrimmons, hereditary pipers to Macleod of Macleod (see Chapter 13). The hereditary standard-bearers, to whom were entrusted the clan's dearest possession, the Fairy Flag, are not buried here, however. They lie with their chiefs at Rodel in Harris. There are several other old graves of interest, including that one which is, according to tradition, *not* the grave of Lady Grange (see Chapter 10).

Of Dunvegan itself there is little to say, for to all intents and purposes Dunvegan virtually means the castle. Every yard of that ancient fortress and lovely modern house has its story.

The drive to the castle, about two miles beyond the hotel, is beautiful, especially in the spring, for the young woods, replanted in the last thirty years, contain a wonderful assortment of trees and shrubs. Here, 'in April, come he will; in May, he sings all day', for these woods are full of cuckoos in the normal way, but after the death of a Macleod chief not a cuckoo can be heard there: they all go to St. Kilda to tell the chief's tenants there that he is dead. As a usual thing cuckoos do not visit St. Kilda, and when even one was heard there its message was well understood. It is on record that after the death of one chief the ship which bore the tidings to St. Kilda found the island already in mourning. But now there is no one left on St. Kilda to whom the birds need carry the news. The St. Kilda folk, and their hens with the strange blue eggs, are scattered throughout Scotland, and what the cuckoos will do in the future I do not know.

Dunvegan Castle is probably the only house in Scotland, perhaps in Britain, to have been inhabited by the same family for over 700 years. The Macleods 'of fire and music' obtained the castle when Leod, the first chief, married the daughter and heiress of Gofra MacRailt, 'King of the Isles', in the thirteenth century, and she brought him the castle on her father's death. Scandal, of course, said he seized it and her, too, and caused her father's sudden end when he and his men came sailing from the north, but there is considerably more evidence that he grew up in Skye as the ward of Paul Baalkason (by some called 'Lord of Skye') and inherited much of his land from him.

Gofra MacRailt—Gofra, son of Harold—is believed to have been of Norse descent, but the name 'Dunvegan' is thought to be of Celtic origin, from Began's Dun, and, if so, it was probably a Celtic fortress before ever the Norsemen landed in Skye. Almost certainly the early Neolithic people of the island would have had a fort on such a rock as Dunvegan even before the Celtic invasions, for those few Skye duns which have been excavated have all shown traces of Stone Age occupation. This is conjecture, however; what is not in doubt is that the Macleods have owned and inhabited the dun since the beginning of the thirteenth century.

Since that day, almost all important visitors to Skye (and many unimportant ones, too!) have visited Dunvegan, from James V in 1540, when he 'persuaded' the chief of his day, Alasdair Crotach, to sail away with him as prisoner or hostage, to Queen Elizabeth and Prince Philip when they lunched at the Castle and planted trees. Dr. Johnson stayed there and wrote warmly of it: indeed, he waxed so enthusiastic that Macleod offered him one of the islands near Dunvegan, Isle Isay, if he would agree to live on it for three months of every year, but the learned doctor would not so far commit himself. Sir Walter Scott, too, slept in the Fairy Room and christened the view from its window 'fairyland'—but would even fairyland be so lovely? In the Fairy Room, as is seemly, fairy music may be heard, and in the Fairy Tower bagpipes are played by no earthly piper.

The castle itself belongs, as might be expected, to many periods. A most interesting account of its architecture is to be read in the *Dunvegan Castle Official Guide*, by W. Douglas Simpson, M.A., D.Litt. It is interesting, too, to note his suggestion that Malcolm, the third chief, who is believed to have married a niece of Robert the Bruce, may have been lent the services of 'a Royal Master Mason', since his addition is 'a most notable piece of architecture'.

Perhaps the best known, and certainly the most precious possession of Clan Macleod is now framed on the wall of the castle drawing-room, once the banqueting hall. This is the Fairy Flag. It is a large silk handkerchief or small banner, brown with age and embroidered with 'elf-spots'. Sir Reginald Macleod took it to the South Kensington Museum on one occasion for expert opinion as to its origin. The considered reply was that it was of Eastern silk and very probably, in their opinion, had been brought back from one of the Crusades as a trophy. The 'elf-spots' were beautiful Eastern darns. 'You believe it to be a relic of the Crusades: *I know* it was given to my ancestor by the fairies', answered Sir Reginald, to which the Curator replied with charming courtesy: 'I bow to your superior knowledge, Sir Reginald!'

The story of the coming of the Flag has many versions. Here is one of them. One of the early chiefs of Dunvegan, Ian the fourth chief or his father Malcolm 'the Fat and Good', is reputed to have married a fairy maid—not an unusual practice at this time. They were very devoted to each other and very happy until her son was born, when the call to return to her own people came to her. Against this order there was never, for her or for others, any appeal. She told her husband that the hour had come and he went with her as far as mortal man might. At Fairy Bridge they said their last goodbye and parted, the chief returning to Dunvegan a lonely man. By the custom of the clan, however, there was soon a great gathering in the castle to celebrate the birth of the heir. While the rejoicings went on, the baby heir, centre and cause of all the feasting and merriment, was completely forgotten, even his nurse having left him to join in the fun below. He soon wriggled off his coverings, as babies will, and waking cold and miserable began to cry. No human being heard him, but his mother did; gentle, unseen hands covered him with a soft silken coverlet, the Fairy Flag, and gentle voices began to sing him back to cosy happiness. The nurse heard the voices. Terrified, she sped to the room and there found him smiling to that which she could not see. She wrapped him in the Flag and so carried him down to the banqueting hall and there told her story. Then fairy voices singing were heard by the chief and all of the clan there assembled. The voices promised that the Flag, if waved in peril or trouble, would bring immediate and powerful help not of this world. Three wavings the clan might have.

The Flag was put carefully away and soon a Standard Bearer was appointed, the office remaining hereditary in one family for nearly 300 years. Usually the Flag (cased) was borne into battle with the clan, the chief and a guard of twelve being sworn to die in its defence. Often its mere presence was enough to turn the tide of war.

Ever after, the baby's nurse sang him to sleep with the fairies' lullaby. Tradition has it she told her descendants that the tune so impressed her when she first heard it that she never forgot a note, but the words she found hard to remember and whenever she hesitated or stopped she would be helped by voices all about her taking up the song. She said, too, that 'her' baby never suffered from any of the small accidents common to the nursery world and she believed that he was always guarded and protected by the fairies. The Dunvegan Cradle Song is unquestionably very old, being written in an ancient, almost forgotten form of Gaelic. It was sung for many generations over the Dunvegan heirs, no woman unable to sing it being chosen as nurse for the young chief. There are various translations of the lullaby. Here are two different authors' versions of the first two verses for comparison.

First Miss Tolmie's:

> *Behold my child, limbed like the roe or fawn,*
> *Smiting the horses,*
> *Seizing the accoutrements of the shod horses,*
> *Of the spirited steeds,*
> *Behold my child.*
>
> *Oh that I could see thy cattle folds,*
> *High up upon the mountain side,*
> *A green shaggy jacket about thy white shoulders,*
> *And a linen shirt,*
> *My little child.*

Then Kenneth Macleod's:

> *Sleep my little child,*
> *Hero, tenderling,*
> *Dream, my little child,*
> *Hero, fawn-like one,*
> *High on mountain brows*
> *Be thy stag tryst,*
> *Speed thy yew arrow straight antlerwards.*
>
> *Sleep my little child,*
> *Hero, gentle-bred,*
> *Dream, my little child,*
> *Hero, battle bred,*
> *Skin like falling snow,*
> *Green thy mail coat,*
> *Live thy steeds, dauntless thy following.*

All are agreed that the Flag has twice, and twice only, been waved in time of crisis and that both times the fairies, as they promised, made all things well for the clan, but there are several different stories of the wavings. There are claims that it has been waved in five different battles, two in Waternish (one of these being the Battle of Trumpan Church), the Battle of Loch Sligachan, the Battle of Bloody Bay, and the Battle of Glendale. It is also said to have been waved to stop a cattle murrain which was devastating the Skye herds, at that time the island's main source of livelihood. The probability seems to be that it really was waved at the Battle of Trumpan Church (see Chapter 10) and on one other occasion, but that at the other battles it was only raised (cased) as a rallying point and inspiration and that this proved sufficient.

For instance, the story goes that at the time of the Battle of Glendale Alasdair Crotach was in Harris when the Macdonalds landed. His mother, a Maclean of Loch Buy, ordered out the castle garrison and also the Fairy Flag. The standard-bearer objected. No one but the chief, he claimed, could order the banner into battle. But the Lady of Macleod of that day was a person of determination, and soon the war galleys were crossing Loch Dunvegan with standard and standard-bearer on board, not to mention the Lady herself. In vain, on arrival, the castle warden begged her to remain with the galleys on the shore; she insisted on being helped up the steep cliff-path and accompanied the party to a hill looking down into the valley. Here she agreed to remain 'temporarily' while the men went into action. The battle swayed back and forth but at length it became obvious that the result would be a Macdonald victory. The Macleods were being pressed back through the pass to their boats. The warden realized that very shortly the Lady of Macleod would be cut off and surrounded on her hill and he sent two trusted men to get her and the Flag away. But the

old lady had quite other views and greeted the message
with a brief 'Nonsense!' She then ordered the standard-
bearer to raise the Fairy Flag (cased), since none but the
chief in person might order its waving. The Macleods became suddenly aware of two facts: first, that the Fairy Flag
was with them, and second, that it and the Lady of Macleod
were in great danger of capture. A supreme effort was made.
Macleods swept forward until Flag and Lady were safely
behind their line and then, fired by an enthusiasm that
nothing could stop, swept on into the valley below just as
the chief, who had landed with the main body of the clan,
came over the hill from Poultiel. Seeing that the day was
won the Lady of Macleod permitted her maid, who had
accompanied her, to help her back to the galleys. All the
same, this battle is sometimes claimed as the first occasion
on which the Flag was actually waved.

As lately as the Second World War, some members of Clan
Macleod went into battle with a photograph of the Fairy
Flag in their pocket-books, and so the Flag, no longer with
a guard of twelve but still an inspiration, flew over Berlin
in the most modern of bombers, landed on the beaches of
Normandy, and grew dusty in the sands of Africa. And
from all over the world Macleods, by name or blood, come
to pay it homage in its island home.

The Flag was also the subject of prophecy—a prophecy
made by Coinneach Odhar (Kenneth Ouir) of the Lews,
who has often been confused with the Brahn Seer. Kenneth,
who lived in the time of Tormod, eleventh Chief of Macleod,
received his gift of second sight thus. Kenneth's mother
was taking her turn one night at watching the cornfields
when an apparition—a woman in water-soaked garments
—appeared and, weeping and lamenting, passed her by.
Realizing that she must be the ghost of a stranger washed

ashore and lately buried near by, the woman was very frightened, for a ghost is bad enough but a strange foreign ghost who may not understand Gaelic is much worse. But pity outweighed fear and she hurried to the empty grave and laid her spindle across it. When the spirit returned, she could not enter and entreated the woman to remove her spindle. 'Tell me first why you weep?' 'Because I cannot rest, for I am a stranger and my grave was never purchased. The dead should have peace', she replied. (A foreigner must buy the right to lie in Highland earth.) 'How can I give you rest?' asked the woman. 'Lay a handful of corn from your husband's fields in my grave', replied the spirit. The woman did so and the ghost lay down in peace. But first she handed a beautiful black stone to the woman who had befriended her and told her to give it to her firstborn son on the seventh anniversary of his birth, neither sooner nor later. This she did, and as soon as he took the stone in his hand he began to prophesy, saying: 'A large whale is ashore in the ravens' cave', and one was.

Kenneth's prophecy with regard to the Flag was as follows (this is only a part of it): 'When Norman, the fourth Norman, the son of the hard, slender, English Lady, should perish by accident; when the Maidens should become the property of a Campbell; when a fox should have her litter in a turret of the Castle: then the Fairy enchanted Banner should be for the last time exhibited and the glory of the Macleod family should depart.' After this, a great part of their lands would be sold, until a currach (small boat) 'would suffice to carry all the gentlemen of the name across Loch Dunvegan'. But in far distant times a chief, Iain Breac, should arise, redeem the estates, and raise the power and honour of the House to an even higher greatness.

Two hundred years later, Norman (the fourth Norman in

succession), son of a southern, English-speaking mother, went down in H.M.S. *Queen Charlotte*; Campbell of Ensor had a tack of Orbost, and so of the Maidens, and a tame fox had a litter in a turret of the castle. At this time, 1799, the chief being from home, his man of business persuaded an English smith to break open the strong box in which the Flag was housed. This he did in the presence of Dr. Norman Macleod of Morven, who was sworn to secrecy but left an account of the whole occurrence, which account is to be read in the *Official Guide to the Castle*. The account includes the names of three persons of note at that day whom Dr. Macleod knew personally to have had copies of the prophecy in their possession prior to its fulfilment. The question now is, did that 'exhibiting' of the banner break the enchantment or has it still the power to save once more ?

Other legends and stories of the Fairy Flag are to be found in the *Official Guide*.

It looks as if some faint but exciting indications of what may prove to be the true history of the Fairy Flag are at last coming to light. They have been found in the sagas concerned with Harald Haardrada. He, it seems, as a young man visited Constantinople, where he joined the Imperial Bodyguard, which he subsequently rose to command, and saw much service in the East, including Jerusalem. He returned to Scandinavia through Russia, where he married the daughter of a Russian Grand Duke, Jaroslav. He came home laden with treasure and used a part of it to buy for himself half the kingdom of Norway from his nephew Magnus. But, according to the sagas, what he valued above all the gold and jewels in his possession was the magic banner Landöda, the Land Ravisher, which, when waved, brought certain victory. When he landed in England and fought with Harold at Stamford Bridge, Landöda was left on board, or so the saga says, though why is not clear, and though it was landed as soon as the tide of battle turned against him it arrived too late to save Harald from the 'seven feet of English earth' promised him by Harold, or his men from total defeat. Here the saga ends, but it does seem as if there might be some connexion between the magic victory-bringing banner of the Northmen and the Fairy Flag of the Norse family of Macleod. Magic swords, spears, and cooking-pots were very common, but these two, if two they be and not one, are the only magic banners that I know of.

Two suggestions have been put forward. One is that the Macleods, who may be descended from Harald Haardrada through the Kings of Man, might have inherited the Flag from one of their Norse ancestors to whom it passed on Harald's death, but this connexion has not yet been established. The second suggestion is that one of Harald Haardrada's descendants may have brought the Flag to Skye in some of their many raids on that island. Skye tradition has it that with the help of the Fiennes, the 'little people' of Skye again and again drove off the sea-pirates, or sometimes drove them into the sea. Might they not have captured the Flag? Then later, when, driven underground into the duns and 'Picts' houses', they had become the Sithe (fairies), might they not, or a maiden of their blood, have in fact brought the magic banner to Dunvegan—perhaps as her dowry, perhaps to bring good fortune to her child, heir alike of the Norse conquerors and the children of the soil who lived in and loved this island before Celts or Norsemen came? Most old 'fairy tales' contain a grain of truth.

It has even been suggested, further, that in the early days whenever the banner went forth to war, out of every sithein and dun bright eyes peered, like rabbits, from a burrow, watching, watching, for the Flag to be waved free. And then, out of their burrows came the great, mysterious armies testified to have been seen 'almost immediately' by the enemy, but whose coming no foe is ever said to have abided. For the fairies were the old inhabitants, and the fairies are usually represented as friendly to Clan Macleod.

As yet the truth is not known, but at last there seems hope that we may one day know the facts.

In the castle drawing-room, not far from the Flag, are preserved Rory Mor's Horn and the Dunvegan Cup. The former, which holds nearly half a gallon, is supposed to be filled with wine and drained at a draught by each successive chief on his coming of age. Like the Flag, the Horn has several legends about its origin, and all connect it with the Macleod of Dunvegan crest, a bull's head, and their motto, 'Hold Fast'.

The first two stories are concerned with Malcolm, the third chief, who must have been a really memorable person. He, it is said, went to pay a state visit to the Earl of Argyll at Inveraray. Here he was entertained most royally with hunting and feasting, but even hunting can pall and so to make a change Argyll suggested that as a member of his clan who had committed some offence was that day to be gored to death by a bull, they might find it more entertaining to watch this spectacle than to take to the hill again. Malcolm agreed. They took their places; man and bull were let into the ring. The man was so fine a specimen and bore himself so bravely that Malcolm was much impressed and, turning to Argyll, said: 'You offered me a gift to commemorate this visit, my Lord Earl; may I pray you to give me that man's life?' 'Gladly would I, if I could', replied Argyll, 'but you have spoken too late. The bull is in the ring and nothing can save him now.' 'If I save him, may I have him?' asked Macleod, and suiting the action to the word vaulted into the arena, caught the bull by the horns, and to cries of 'Hold fast, Macleod, hold fast', with one mighty heave flung it to the ground. In my childhood one family in Dunvegan was still pointed out as being descended from the rescued Campbell.

Another version makes Malcolm slay, with his bare hands, a wild bull which attacked him in the forests of Glenelg. He had been paying a clandestine visit to the wife of Clan Fraser's chief. Unfortunately she heard of this feat and was so thrilled by it that she left her husband and joined Malcolm at Dunvegan, thereby starting a lengthy clan war.

In both these cases Malcolm is supposed to have brought back the horn as a trophy.

The third version is now almost forgotten and concerns Rory Mor, whose horn it is said to have been. He, as a young man, was supervising some agricultural operation for his brother William, the twelfth chief, when the beacon fires were seen to blaze. Realizing that Macdonalds had probably landed and that haste was imperative, Rory led his men up to a herd of cattle grazing near, and seizing the bull by its horns, sprang on to its back and, crying to his men to mount the cows and 'hold fast', he stampeded the herd in the direction of Dunvegan. They arrived in time to join William's force and rout the enemy. The bull that had carried him so well was given a safe-conduct for life and a pension payable in fodder, and at its death its horn, silver-mounted, became the Horn of Rory Mor.

The Dunvegan Cup is believed to be of Irish origin and very old. Round the brim is an inscription which says that the cup was made in 1493 for Katherine, daughter of

King Neil and wife of Macguire, Prince of Fermanagh. The actual wooden cup, however, made probably of bog oak, is believed to be much older than its silver mountings and traditionally belonged to Niall Glun Dubh (Neil of the Black Knees) who was King of Ulster in the tenth century and an ancestor of Katherine's. There is good evidence that one of the O'Neills visited Rory Mor at Dunvegan, after that chief had led 500 men to help him against Elizabeth of England, and brought a gift of a 'beautiful cup'. It is generally believed that this is the one. The silver setting, inscribed with a text, was much ornamented both with Celtic patterns and with coral and semi-precious stones, though many of the latter are now missing. (For legends of the coming of the cup, see Chapters 12 and 17.)

In the Muniment Room are many charters conveying gifts from kings, and many letters bearing royal seals, for in past days Macleod corresponded as an equal with the kings both of England and of Scotland. But the letter that holds a place of honour on the wall was not written by a king. It was written by tenants and crofters on the estate in 1777, at a time when, the estate being much impoverished, it was feared that the then Macleod would have to sell much of his land. It declared their intention of raising their own rents by a shilling and sixpence in the pound in an effort to avoid this catastrophe. Later, the help that his grandson gave them in the famine years ruined him and sent him south to work. It is sometimes well to remember that there *was* another side to that period which it is now fashionable to mention only in connexion with the Evictions. Evictions there were, and most wicked ones; bad and absentee landlords there were, but that they were not the only ones, though naturally the most 'memorable', is shown by the attitude of overseas Macleods to their chief today, which seems to suggest that hatred was not the emotion which *their* ancestors, at any rate, carried with them into the New World.

Just before the last war, in November 1938, one small seventeenth-century wing of the castle, the Iain Breac wing, was destroyed by fire. The nine-foot walls of the old keep cared little for what the flames could do, but the interior of that wing was destroyed. Fortunately it was found possible to replace the burnt part so exactly that, but for such things as a modern kitchen, no one would notice any change. Fortunately, too, it was finished before the war-time building restrictions began—but only just.

On the night of the fire not only was every able-bodied man from Dunvegan there to help, but cars and lorries came, crammed with helpers, from farther and farther afield as the news spread until, by dawn, it seemed all Skye was there. Then came the rain.

All furniture, pictures, and treasures (except from the wing where the fire began) had been saved and were stacked outside. What to do with them was the question. But by the time those in charge stopped rescuing and began to think of storing there was nothing left to store. Everything had been loaded into cars, lorries, and buses or carts and just vanished. When the insurance men arrived, they tore their hair. 'Priceless treasures. May be in America by now.' But their owner refused to be in the least perturbed. They had to be got out of the rain, she pointed out reasonably, and that was the only way it could be done quickly. 'They'll all come back as soon as we let it be known we are ready to store them.' And they did, down to the last teaspoon and pillow-slip.

On one of the islands which can be seen from the castle windows (the Colbost Islands) there used to be traces of a ruined building, though whether it was a watch-tower or a monk's cell appears to be a moot point. But in medieval times the monks supported the legend of Scotia, daughter of the King of Egypt, and of how she came with her husband, Prince Gathelus, and his following, first to Spain, then to Ireland, and eventually to Scotland, whence its name. The chiefs in the Islands and Highlands, however, held other views as to their origin. But as in the Skye version of the legend Scotia visits not only Skye but Dunvegan Loch, it looks as if there might once have been a monkish settlement there, and one not above a little propaganda. For Scotia became a Christian and, leaving her husband and his kin fighting in Spain, she joined St. Joseph of Arimathæa on his wondrous and miraculous voyage. Their boat was a stone—that stone which was first Jacob's pillow, later closed the Holy Sepulchre, and is now the Stone of Destiny. In this strange boat they sailed to Ireland, naturally meeting with many adventures on the journey: here the Stone rested on the Hill of Tara for a time and was called Innisfoil (Stone of Fortune). Then it grew restless and became a boat once more, in which they sailed on, first to Skye, where the Stone came ashore at the foot of the castle rock in Loch Dunvegan and the Stone (not Scotia or St. Joseph) blessed the rock with 'the blessing of permanence for itself and all that grew upon it' before it passed on to touch at Iona and land at last in Argyll.

In this Loch Dunvegan, too, is another supernatural stone, the Rocabarra (Stone of the sea-tangle top) which has twice appeared to human sight (once being to salute St. Columba): when it appears for the third time the destruction of the world will be imminent. 'When Rocabarra appears again, the world is due for destruction' is the say-

ing. But to some, Rocabarra was the Island of the Blest
and its last appearance would be the coming of the earthly
paradise.

It is well known that in most Skye lochs a suicide would
drive away fish and that a man who had woman's blood
on his hands need never again go fishing, for the fish know.
Herring, however, are even more particular and will not
enter the net of any boat aboard which there is a murderer
or man of violence (battle and war are exempted) for herring fear blood and fly from it. But then, herring always
were queer fish and live on the foam of their own tails. In
Dunvegan Loch there are always fish in plenty as long as
the chief is in residence, but let him depart—even for a
day—and the fish go with him. They disappear, too, if any
woman other than a Macleod crosses from Dunvegan to the
nearest island.

If any danger or trouble threatens Macleod of Macleod,
balls of fire can be seen dancing high in the air over Dunvegan Loch and the castle rock itself. Then there are the
'swan folk'; these appear sometimes as wild swans, sometimes as soft white clouds. Normally they pass over the
castle and other Macleod land, including Orbost, Bracadale, Struan, and some say Gesto (but *not* Uiginish) every
five years. Anyone of Macleod name or blood seeing them
as they fly low to bless the castle will have good fortune.
Should the chief or his heir be a baby at the time of such a
visit, and alone, the swans will pause in their 'good flight'
to play with him. This, too, brings good fortune. It is
curious that the swans' flight appears to follow such parts
of the Macleod lands as have duns upon them, just as in
mainland districts swans are associated with crannochs
and ancient burial mounds.

The best view of the castle from the land is to be had

from the road that runs on past it to Claggan Farm and the Coral Beach. Not a car road all the way, or indeed any of the way, but a most lovely walk and possible for a strong-minded car. On this Coral Beach are found the small cowries which bring happiness and good fortune. To aid them in this good work, however, it is necessary for the finder to return to the beach a year to the day after collecting them and to throw them back, one by one, into the sea.

The Coral Beach is a beautiful sight, being entirely covered with snow-white coral sand and small lumps of coral. F. Fraser Darling says that it is not true coral at all but a form of seaweed, *Lithothamnion.* Such a blow! However, the sand is so very like in appearance to the coral sand of the true coral islands in the West Indies and it reflects so much light that the sun seems always shining there and one can lie back and bask in the sunshine (real or pretended) on the coral (real or pretended) and, watching the seals at play, pretend with no difficulty at all that it is, as was long believed, the one and only true coral beach in Britain.

12

Glendale

———•■•———

In the dark nights of winter
Round the peat fire we gathered;
With song, tale and laughter
The hours we would pass.
Tales of great men long gone
Were then told us by the old ones:
Proud we still of their glory
In my childhood's lovely glen.

(From 'Glendale', by Neil Macleod, translated)

GLENDALE, as its name from the Gaelic word Gleann
meaning a Glen and the Norse word Dalr meaning a Dale
implies, is not a town but a valley. It is separated from the
rest of Skye by one of the worst hills in the island, and
this hill has probably had more to do with the history of
the district than any other single factor, for during many
long centuries—indeed, until cars became the ordinary
means of transport—it was an almost complete barrier
cutting the glen off from the rest of Skye. Of course, in
early days in the Highlands, the sea or other water was the
usual highway, horse transport being a very secondary
matter, and this continued in Glendale until the last few
years. Supplies came direct to Poultiel Pier by a regular
steamer service; visitors came and left by the same route,
knowing little of the rest of the island, even Dunvegan.
So Glendale was a place apart and, as is apt to happen in
such circumstances, there grew up there a very fine and
independent race of men. The girls were famous alike for

their looks, their quick intelligence, and their extraordinary gift for arranging flowers, usually the only outlet for their undoubted artistic gifts. Glendale had, too, the good fortune to have a quite exceptional schoolmaster for many years. Even today Glendale is different, for the people now are not just crofters, but the joint owners of that large estate which they joined together to buy. Like most pioneers, however, they have their troubles, for ownership in these days of heavy taxation has its own drawbacks.

The road to Glendale branches off the Dunvegan–Roag road to the right, about half a mile beyond Lonmore Church, and runs through undulating moorland until it crosses the Osdale river. Beyond this lovely brown trout-stream two roads take off to the right, the first leading back to Dunvegan via the Manse of Duirinish, on whose knoll the fairies dance, the second to Uiginish, the castle dower-house, which faces Dunvegan across the waters of the loch. To the left of the main road, before the Uiginish road leaves it, lies Dun Osdale, which some claim to be the original home of the famous Dunvegan Cup. Here is the story.

One midsummer night a Macleod, searching for strayed cattle, stayed late on the moor. In the moonlight he saw the door of Dun Osdale open and the Little People come out, a long train of them, and begin to dance on the green grass knoll near by. Fascinated, he watched, forgetting everything but the wonderful dance. Suddenly he sneezed. The spell was broken. The dance stopped. Macleod sprang up to fly, but the fairies were upon him and he was dragged, willy-nilly, into the dun. Inside, as soon as his eyes grew accustomed to that strange green light associated with fairyland, he beheld a pleasing sight. A great banquet was spread on a large table carved from a single tree: on it were vessels of gold and silver, many of them set with jewels or chased in strange designs. His fairy 'hosts' led him to the table, poured wine into one of the beautiful cups and, giving it to him, invited him to toast their chief. Now this man's mother was a witch, so he knew well that if he ate or drank in the Dun he was in the Daoine Sithe's power for ever. He lifted the cup and appeared to drink the required toast but in fact skilfully let the wine run down inside his coat. As soon as his neighbours saw the cup was half empty they ceased to bother about him but went off on their own affairs or to attend the banquet. Thereafter Macleod watched for a chance of escape and, when one offered, slipped quietly through the door of the dun and away, carrying the cup with him. The fairies soon realized what had happened and started in pursuit but he was already across the Osdale river and in safety. He hurried home told his mother the story, and showed her the cup. Being a wise woman she realized the peril in which he undoubtedly stood and at once put her most powerful spell upon him to protect him from the arts of the Daoine Sithe, warning him seriously never to leave the house for a moment without getting the spell renewed. But she forgot to put a protecting spell upon the cup also. The fairies soon discovered the exact state of affairs and immediately laid their own spell upon the cup, a spell so powerful that all who saw the cup, or even heard of it, were seized with an overmastering de-sire to possess it, even if such possession involved the murder of the holder. For a year all went well and thanks to his mother's care the young man went unharmed. Then he grew careless and one day ventured out without the protecting spell. A one-time friend, bewitched by the cup, had been awaiting just such a chance and immediately murdered him and went off with the prize. The fairies, their revenge achieved, took no further interest in the matter, but Macleod of Macleod did. The boy's mother hurried to him with her story and he at once gave orders that the murderer be found and brought to justice. He was duly hanged and the trouble-making cup, now free of enchantment, passed into the possession of the chief and can still be seen in the castle. This story is also told of other duns in the vicinity. The authentic account of the cup's origin and its journeying from Ireland can be found in the *Official Guide to Dunvegan Castle*.

Soon the road, with beautiful views of Dunvegan Loch, the castle, and the Colbost Islands, reaches the township of Skinidin. According to Forbes's *Place Names of Skye*, Skinidin, the 'bleached or withered Dun', is one of four duns which guarded the peninsula at this spot, the others being known in Gaelic as the Round Dun, the Long Dun, and the Short Dun, but little, if any, trace of these old forts still remains. A nunnery, too, is said once to have graced this spot, then known as 'The Shieling of the Women'. All this coast is thick with Gaelic names, each commemorating some event in the district's past, for Dunvegan Loch is one with a long history in a land of long memories. At Colbost, about a mile beyond Skinidin, the road splits into two, the right-hand fork leading through Totaig to Borreraig and Galtrigal while the left-hand or main road carries on into Glendale.

This left-hand fork at once begins to rise sharply, for this is *the* hill. Passing Colbost School on its right, it skirts a small but grim and desolate little valley. Above this valley stands Beinn na Creiche (Plunder Mount), on whose summit the spoil taken after the Battle of the Aird, two miles away, is said to have been divided. The road continues to mount until on reaching the summit, spread out below it like a life-size map lies the Valley of Glendale. This largest and most fertile valley in Skye is dotted with crofts and small townships as far as one can see, and through its heart runs the Hamara river, once the carver of the land-scape.

As one would suppose, such a fertile and desirable land did not go unnoticed by the Fiennes, that giant race which inhabited Skye when all the world was young. It was here they fed their grey goats and also their famous cow Glas Ghoillean (Grey Shoulders), who gave eleven gallons at each milking and was a great talker, having human speech. An old Gaelic verse gives her four favourite pasturages as 'Gleanndail an Duirinish, Gleann Uig an Trotternish, Gleann Sgiamhach Sgaladail, and Gleann Aluinn Romas-dail'. And not a bad choice either. Tradition has it that as she chewed the cud she thought much and produced as a result many Gaelic proverbs which, when the old 'Proverb Game' was played at winter ceilidhs, were frequently quoted. Whether it was due to the wisdom of her proverbs or to a wisdom natural to the soil, it is certain that the people of Glendale not only were leaders in 'The Rising', better known perhaps as the 'crofter agitation' in the 80's, but came well out of it.

It is a characteristic story. The crofters of that time suf-fered under many most unjust impositions and the days of the Evictions, with their bitterness, were not forgotten, so discontent grew up all over the island. In particular there was strong feeling in Glendale, Trotternish, and the Braes, and meetings on 'Land Reform' were held at Fairy Bridge. In Glendale the leader of the unrest was John Macpherson of Milivaig and he was, in fact, imprisoned for some of his acts, but by then his campaign was almost won. It is said that the Staffin leader sent him a message: 'Stretch the law but do not break it', but that he did not take this advice.

In the Braes, however, the people started a fight with police sent to evict some of them who had refused to pay their rents. This was the 'Battle of the Braes', an action which could only (and did) result in reinforcements, troops, and bitter feeling. Glendale was wiser. The authorities, alarmed by the 'Battle of the Braes', decided that Glendale would be even more dangerously rebellious. It was, they thought, unsafe to send police or even troops but that under the guns of a man-of-war marines could be landed, so a ship of the Royal Navy steamed into Loch Poultiel. They found Glendale ready for them. When a party of marines and bluejackets came ashore they saw on the road above the harbour a large crowd of people welcoming them with cheers. As they advanced they were greeted by the hearty singing of 'God Save the Queen', followed by a speech of welcome in which it was made clear that now the Navy had arrived Glendale was safe and happy, for that flag stood for justice all the world over and they knew that now justice would be done.

The young officer in command was somewhat embarrassed and hardly knew what to do. He and his men had landed with bayonets fixed and every preparation to withstand a hail of stones and broken bottles, but the only use they could find for the bayonets was to hang their caps on them when entertained to lunch at Hamara Lodge. The marks of the bayonets were long preserved in the wall there. The only bottles they saw were those connected with a strictly unofficial shabeen in the hills, to which the marines paid strictly unofficial visits as welcome guests. His report naturally was of a most loyal people and some obvious misunderstanding or injustice. It is true that John Macpherson, the 'Glendale Martyr', went to prison for a time, but out of Glendale's wisdom and other circumstances came the Crofters' Act and much good. The Glendale Martyr, too, received compensation in the form of a subscription from sympathizers both in and outside Skye. With these subscriptions he was able to open a shop in the district, which was said to have caused a certain loss of popularity in some quarters.

But to return to the road. It descends the hill (too steep for safety in times of ice and snow) to Hamara river. Half-way down on the right a road takes off. Passing the church and the manse with its fir trees it runs through the townships of Glasvein and Ferrinequire and across the hill to Borreraig. This is one of the loveliest drives, and worst roads, in Skye.

Ferrinequire is said to mean Macquarrie's Land, i.e. Land of Godfrey's Son, and to have got its name from being granted as his 'portion' to a son of Godfrey, Lord of the Isles. If so, he must have come off badly in the matter of inheritance since, though Macdonalds landed in Glendale on more than one occasion, I am not aware that they ever successfully held land there. Certainly the Battle of Glendale in 1490 was not a Macdonald victory, thanks to that 'Lady of Macleod' who in her son's absence herself accompanied such men as she could muster in haste to Glendale to repel the invaders.[1]

Beside Hamara river not far from the bridge lies Kilchoan graveyard and the ruins of the old church of Kilchoan. The last service was held there about 200 years ago, but now only the outline of the little church is to be seen. The font or holy-water stoup has, however, been preserved and can still be seen there. Kilchoan was one of the original parish

[1] See *Tales of Dunvegan*, by Brenda Macleod.

churches of Skye, later, but probably not much later, than those founded by St. Columba, and it was dedicated to St. Congan or Comgal, son of a king of Leinster and brother of the better-known St. Kentigern. Congan is believed to have been of the Iona ministry and to have had his 'cell' where the church stood. Tradition has it that he was that same St. Comgal who, with St. Canice, accompanied St. Columba when he first landed in Scotland and paid his famous visit to King Brude at Inverness. Later this St. Comgal quarrelled with St. Columba over a church and their respective kinsfolk in Ireland (St. Columba was of the Hy Neill and St. Comgal of the Dal-Araidhe) fought a great battle on behalf of the two saints. At the end of his life St. Comgal founded the monastery of Bangor in Ireland and became a successful abbot.

In the ruins of Kilchoan Church a twisted elder-tree grows. This tree, according to tradition, grows out of the grave of a Scandinavian prince named Diel or Tiel. He was a great prince of Norway, it is thought the king's son, and he came with his ships of war to Scotland. He was killed in battle or, as some have it, drowned, and his ships sailed into the bay bringing his body for burial in the little church of Kilchoan, but first they laid the body down on the shore, where a skerry is still known as Cnoclannach, the Norseman's Skerry. The bay, till then known as Loch-a-Chuain, Loch of the Ocean, became Poltiel or Poultiel, Pool or Mud of Tiel. Within living memory an old man in the district found that he could not keep his sheep out of his cabbages, so one night in the dark he came to the graveyard and cut billets out of the elder tree to protect his cabbages. This became known and John Macleod, brother of Neil Macleod the Skye Bard, wrote certain verses lampooning him. What they were is known only to Glendale, for they were never

published. They had, however, the desired effect: no one
since has dared to harm the tree.

Among those buried in the graveyard in more recent
times was Donald Macleod, a noted bard, the father of John
and Neil. Among the gravestones is one medieval one,
carved with a sword and the usual Celtic designs commonly
seen on the gravestones of Iona. No one knows its history
nor whom it commemorates though its date, in Roman
numerals, was legible some forty years ago.

The road winds on up the long hill out of the valley on
the farther side, past Hamara Lodge in its wood and past
Borrodale School. Here a road takes off left-handed to
Waterstein Lighthouse. Waterstein can boast some of the
wildest scenery and steepest cliffs in Skye. It is well worth
a visit—preferably in storm, when it is magnificent. Near
it is Neist Point, made famous by the Brahn Seer who
prophesied that one day a rock called Cnogan, Rock of the
large Dog Whelks, should fall into the sea with 'as many
Stewarts as could get a footing on it'. The rock is already in
the sea, however, and as far as is known got there without
harm to Clan Stewart—but, of course, it might still turn
over, for anything might happen in Camas nan Sithean,
the Fairies' Bay.

The main road continues through crofts and a wonderful
display of wild flowers, some unknown elsewhere in Skye,
till it drops suddenly as a stone down to Poultiel Pier.
Loch Poultiel is a grand and beautiful bay with high cliffs
on either hand, down which on calm days waterfalls drop
straight into the sea below but in certain winds they 'fall'
upwards instead of down and ultimately dissolve in smoke
above the cliff tops. It has to be seen to be believed. In
the bay are several small rocks usually covered with scarts
and puffins, busy about their own fishy affairs, while solan

geese can be counted upon to give a more spectacular display.

The road again rises sharply to reach Upper and Lower Milivaig, two townships which appear literally to be at the end of the Old World, with only America beyond. It was in one of these that the 'Glendale Martyr' was born, and from them wonderful views of the Outer Islands can be had.

13

Borreraig

Nature's voice heard by them, chief among pipers
Caught and held fast by them, set here for ever,
The sea-voice and hill-voice and moor-voice of Scot-
*   land.*
In the pibrochs of Skye on the Pipes of MacCrimmon.

(Composed, for the unveiling of the MacCrimmon
    memorial, by Charles Richard Cammell)

THE road to Borreraig leaves the Glendale road at Colbost
and runs along the steep hillside through the townships of
Totaig and Uig, to drop steeply into the little valley where
Husabost House lies in the trees. Here the road passes a
ruined barn, once the chapel of St. Francis, and a forgotten
graveyard, which is curious in that tradition places it on a
mound or dun, Cnoc na Cille (Church Mound), like the old
burial cairns, rather than in the usual patch of low ground.

From here the road winds steeply up again to the township of Borreraig; this is a most beautiful stretch of road in
early June when the loveliness of an English spring joins
that of a Skye summer. The road then becomes a lane of
gold, the air heavy with the scent of gorse and the grass beyond blue with wild hyacinths. To the left is the steep Skye
hillside, to the right the deep blue of Loch Dunvegan merg-
ing at last into the still deeper blue of the Outer Isles.
Tradition has it that in the dim ages, before the Norman
Conquest, it was planned to build Dunvegan Castle here on
a promontory still known as the Castle Rock.

Borreraig, though so small a township, is famous not only in Skye but all over the New World as the home of piping, for here the MacCrimmons had their college which it was the ambition of every would-be piper to attend. Many have wondered about the origin of the MacCrimmon family and such absurd suggestions as Italians shipwrecked in Skye have been put forward to account for their musical genius. The Bannatyne MS. says that the family held part of south Harris and the islands in the Sound before Paul Baalkason's ancestors conquered that part of the country. As Paul himself died early in the thirteenth century and his people are reputed to have come with the first Norse invaders of the Isles, this would make the MacCrimmons descendants of some of the earliest inhabitants of the West, closely akin to the Mediterranean peoples, but I know of no evidence to support this.

Tradition accounts for their undoubted gifts as follows. It is said that the first MacCrimmon, though a good and worthy piper, was uninspired. He was piper to Macleod of Macleod and also held piping classes on his 'Piper's Land' at Borreraig. He had many pupils, among them his own son. One day MacCrimmon told the boys that Macleod of Macleod wished to choose an assistant piper and would hear them play, each in turn, and choose the best. They all began to practise eagerly, the keenest of all being young MacCrimmon. He took his pipes to the little green knoll at Borreraig which looks out over the loch to the Outer Isles and there practised and practised, but to no purpose, for music was not in him. He himself realized the fact at last; being very young and most bitterly disappointed, he flung down his pipes and, casting himself on the heather beside them, began to weep. Immediately, he saw the knoll open and a lovely lady approached and asked his trouble. He,

usually a very shy youth, found it easy to confide his hopes
and disappointment to her. 'Which would you rather', she
asked, 'pipe badly but be acclaimed great or be a great
piper even if unrecognized?' The boy thought it over carefully, which seemed to please her, and then said: 'I would
like to be a great piper but I can't.' Thereupon the lady
handed him a silver chanter and bade him play it to her.
He did so and found that music, finer than he had ever
imagined, flowed from it. 'When you are merry, all shall
dance; when you are sad, all shall weep', said the lady.
'And when I call you, wherever you are or whatever you
have, you must leave all and come to me. That is the price.
Is it too high?' Again young MacCrimmon thought it over
seriously, then he agreed.

He first played his precious chanter in front of Macleod
of Macleod and his guests in the great hall of Dunvegan.
All were astonished and delighted. He was chosen assistant
piper by acclaim and in due course became hereditary piper
to Macleod of Macleod and head of the Borreraig college,
which he made world-famous. In course of time he married
and had a family, his sons inheriting his gift. Then one day,
when the youngest had become a man, the call which
MacCrimmon had long awaited came. He gave his pipes to
his eldest son (they are now preserved in Dunvegan Castle)
said farewell to his wife and children, and set off, playing
his silver chanter, the fairy's gift, to the great cave at Harlosh. He was never seen again (see Chapter 15). Another
version makes the fairy place a taboo on the chanter, saying that no matter what might go wrong, MacCrimmon
must never blame or abuse it. One day Macleod was voyag-
ing to Harris in his galley when a storm arose and he bade
MacCrimmon play his pipes to hearten the rowers. Mac-
Crimmon attempted to obey but the ship rolled and pitched,

standing became almost impossible, and at last the chanter slipped from his numb, wet fingers and, letting out a dismal shriek, rapped him over the knuckles as it swung. Irritated beyond endurance, MacCrimmon exclaimed: 'Oh, . . . the chanter!' Instantly the little silver chanter detached itself from the pipes and, rising in the air, was last seen flying Skyewards through the storm.

MacCrimmon's descendants remained pipers to Macleod of Macleod until the '45. The MacCrimmon of that day, from a sense of duty, accompanied his chief and the small party which Macleod led to oppose the Prince. MacCrimmon was convinced that he would never return and as the boat made its way across the loch which he was never to see again he composed the famous 'MacCrimmon's Lament'. Many translations of the Lament have been made: here are some lines from that by John Stuart Blackie:

> *Round Coolin's peak the mist is sailing,*
> *The Banshee croons her note of wailing,*
>
> .   .   .   .   .
>
> *The warblers, the soul of the groves, are moaning*
> *For MacCrimmon that's gone with no hope of returning.*

Refrain:

> *No more, no more, no more for ever,*
> *In war or peace, shall return MacCrimmon;*
> *No more, no more, no more for ever,*
> *Shall love or gold bring back MacCrimmon.*

In due course the party saw some fighting in a skirmish about Moy Hall. Only one man was injured in the fight. It was MacCrimmon and he was killed outright. No other member of the party lost his life in the campaign. So ended the MacCrimmon Pipers and College, though a descendant still lives at Borreraig on the old 'Piper's Land'. A monument to the MacCrimmons now stands where young Mac-Crimmon once played and despaired on the fairy knoll, and a piping contest in their memory now takes place there every year.

Borreraig has a possession unique in Skye, and probably in Scotland: this is the Manners Stone, a great stone or small rock situated about a mile beyond the township. The Rev. W. H. Forbes in his *Place Names of Skye* says of it: 'Celtic politeness was enforced here, in a peculiar and drastic manner.' Tradition has it that anyone who walks three times to this stone and rests upon it will 'find their manners'. Perhaps it once took the place of the ducking-stool for village scolds, but now it is the children only who look for their manners there—and certainly they find them. Dalrymple in his memoirs (1700–50) says: 'The Highlanders, whom more savage nations call savage, carry, in the outward expression of their manners, the politeness of courts without their vices, and, in their bosoms, the high point of honour without its follies.'

Beyond Borreraig lies the now tiny township of Galtrigal, but it, too, has a claim to fame, for from it came the Prince's pilot, Donald Macleod. He it was who, after Culloden, risked his life to get the Prince away into safety. Donald Macleod was a well-to-do trader who was visiting Inverness on business when the Jacobite army first entered that town. As he was known to be an honest man and a keen Jacobite, he was approached with a request to arrange the transport of a certain hoard of gold coins from Barra to Moidart. This he did. Shortly after Culloden he met and took charge of the Prince. In this he was aided by his son, a boy of fifteen, who had run away from school in Inverness to fight for the Prince. Donald got the Prince safely to the Long Island and later to Uist. From 21 April to 21 June, when he handed him on to Flora Macdonald, Donald Macleod had the sole responsibility for the Prince's safety. But when the facts became known Donald, having seen him safely into Flora's care, went off alone to draw the hunt. He was captured in Benbecula by Allan Macdonald of Knock in Sleat. He spent many months on a prison ship where conditions were so bad that when he was released in 1747 he returned to Galtrigal a dying man.

But now Galtrigal has fallen upon evil times and only a few houses at the Borreraig end are inhabited; about a mile beyond them lies the remainder of this township. It is now a ruin, peopled only by ghosts, and reminds one irresistibly of Kipling's 'Letting in the Jungle'. For here, too, the houses were left in good condition and it is the wild, growing things which have taken possession. It was abandoned because its peat moor lies below it and at some little distance, and to it no road runs, so that every bit of fuel needed by these crofts had to be carried home on the backs of the inhabitants, and uphill at that. For many generations they struggled on, being, as most Skye townships are, almost entirely self-supporting, growing their own food and food for their beasts, cutting their own peat for fuel, spinning, weaving, and knitting their own garments, and indeed troubling the dollar but little. There they reared their families, fine men and women who have served the Empire in every sphere, but always they were hoping for a little road, perhaps a mile and a half long, and for piped water. But these things never came and so the people are gone.

The story is told of Darius I of Persia, who ruled a great empire, that he desired to find out which of all the peoples over whom he ruled were the finest and best race, that he might encourage them. So he set out, suitably accompanied, to ride throughout his empire. In his travels he met many peoples and many claimants to the honour of being the finest race, but he was not satisfied. So, much to the annoyance of his courtiers, he rode on and on. One day as he was passing through a lonely and wild countryside, he saw before him a woman with a baby in her arms. As he looked he saw that she was carrying a water-pot on her head, leading a goat by a string over her arm, and suckling her baby. 'Now we can go home', said the king, 'for I have found the finest race. If the women can do three things at once, what must the men be like?'

If this be the criterion, it is a pity that Britain is not searching for her finest race today, for it is still possible in Skye to meet a woman carrying peats or hay on her back, driving her cows in front of her, and knitting as she walks so as not to waste time. She may even add practising a song for good measure. And surely to such a people a few road repairs and some piped water might be granted.

14

Dunvegan to the Maidens

Sail round the cliffy West,
And, rising out of the main,
You there shall see the Maidens three,
Like Choosers of the Slain;
And go wherever you may,
With a new and deep surprise,
The Coolin blue will fill your view
And fix your gazing eyes.

('The Isle of Skye', by Alexander Nicolson)

T H I S is a drive-plus-walk well worth taking; there is a public road as far as Orbost, then comes a private road to Varkasaig, and after that only a footpath.

The road to Orbost runs by the foot of Macleod's Tables. No one who has visited Dunvegan is likely to forget the view of them across the Loch, dark against the evening sky or, in calm weather, the reflection in the sea of these two beautiful flat-topped mountains. But Healaval Beg and Healaval More were not always flat-topped. When St. Columba came to convert Skye to Christianity he followed his unvarying practice of going first to visit the chief of each district and ask his permission to preach to his followers before he or his monks began to do so. And so, in due course, he came to the shores of Loch Bracadale, where the chief of the district was then living in a dun by the sea. There are various versions of his journey and of which dun he visited. Whichever it was, the saint was not well received. Probably the chief considered that the son of a brother chief who chose to preach rather than to fight was a poor thing, little better than a renegade. However, St. Columba was given permission to preach one sermon to the chief and his friends, and he chose as his text: 'The foxes have holes and the birds of the air have nests, but the Son of Man hath not where to lay his head', appealing, no doubt, to that sense of hospitality common even then in the Highlands. But as soon as the sermon ended, the chief, a hard man who feared such an appeal might influence his followers, bade him begone, crying: 'Neither fox hole nor nest nor bed nor board shall you and yours find on my land.' And at his command, but with no little effort and noise, the great door of the dun was pushed open so that Columba and his monks might depart. Then above the grating of the gate came another sound, a loud roaring rumble as the earth rocked and the sky grew dark with dust. The startled warriors and the saint hurried out together and as the air cleared they saw, where two pointed hills had been two flat-topped hills stood now. Wiser than the little men at their feet, they offered to God's servant their flattened tops to be his bed and his table.

The name 'Macleod's Table' came later. A Macleod chief visited the King's court in Edinburgh and was, naturally, impressed by much of the grandeur and new ways he saw. One night there was a banquet at which all drank well if not wisely, and a mainland lord began to taunt the islander with remarks such as: 'You never saw such a large table as this in the Islands' or 'Did you ever see such candlesticks [pointing to enormous gold candelabra] in Skye?' 'How do you entertain your guests in Skye? Have you such a hall as this?' At last Macleod grew angry and exclaimed: 'If you do me the honour to visit me at Dunvegan I will show you a larger table and far finer candlesticks than any here, and a better banqueting hall, too, than this one.'

'A wager, a wager': a dozen voices took up the cry. And: 'I accept', said the mainland lord. 'I will visit you at Dunvegan one year from today.' 'And I', 'And I', added others. 'We will accompany him and judge.' 'You will all be welcome', replied Macleod with dignity.

Shortly afterwards Macleod returned to Skye, possibly feeling a little foolish but, if so, quite determined that no one should know it. A year later to the day, his guests arrived and were hospitably received. 'Let us see your table, your candlesticks, your banqueting hall that are finer than the king's', they urged. 'Tonight we will dine', replied Macleod. That night he led the way, up a newly smoothed track, to the summit of Healaval Beg: there, on Macleod's Table, a feast was spread and around it and behind each guest stood stalwart young men of the clan holding aloft flaming torches to light the guests. 'This is my table', said Macleod. 'Can the King in his city show a larger one?' 'These are my candlesticks; brave and faithful followers are worth more than gold. As for my banqueting hall, I dine beneath the canopy of Heaven. Can King James claim a finer ceiling, can the rarest painting equal the stars of God?' Fortunately it appears to have been a fine night.

The road runs on through undulating moorland. All this moor country is good peat ground, and peat-cutting and drying is the chief June work there. A very hard and laborious task it is, especially in a wet season, but enlivened not a little for the younger people by the big 'picnics' of friends and neighbours which are a part of it. In the late autumn and winter, when the deer grass turns red, the moor is a sheet of flame under the setting sun, rivalling an English poppy field. A little later, and 'fairy curtains' of icicles adorn each peat hag, while in the early summer the acres of white bog cotton dancing over the peat bogs rival its winter beauty. It is easy to imagine St. Bride moving among the cotton with her bird, the oyster-catcher, or Page of Bride, crying over her head, busy gathering those armfuls destined to be a bed for little, tired children, and causing it to flourish wherever she passes.

In my mother's childhood bog-cotton heads were a crop like any other, but one mostly gathered by the children. Dried, it was used to stuff pillows and quilts. The heads used whole were apt to become lumpy, but those who had the time and energy to remove the tough base and use only the 'beard' had quilts light and soft as swansdown; it was also spun like linen.

About two miles from the Glendale turning a small grass-grown road takes off to the right and leads to two ruined crofts, once two pleasant little homes, known as Croc-na-Sca. In one of these lived an old woman, Mary Ann Mac-leod, who had second sight. Her visions usually took the form of dreams which very frequently came true. The night my maternal grandfather (John Robertson of Orbost) died in 1904, she dreamed a dream. She said that she saw my father riding in from the sea on a white horse. He came ashore at Varkasaig and rode his horse up the road to Orbost, up the front steps of the house and into the hall. After a minute or two he rode out again and over to the steading, where he dismounted and stabled his horse in token of possession. Then he vanished. She told this dream to many people and said that they would see that sooner or later he and his would own Orbost. When, forty years later, my husband and I bought it from my uncle's execu-tors, the dream was still remembered.

The next thing that happens upon the road is a very

sharp, almost right-angle, turn to the left. This is the main road through Roag to Bracadale. The road which leads straight on to Orbost and Varkasaig is a private one. But the way to the Maidens lies straight on. The road very shortly passes Orbost House, silhouetted against sky and sea, with, from its windows, one of the most beautiful, if not *the* most beautiful view in Skye. Those who built it must have appreciated the fact, for, like Mr. Punch's celebrated hotel at the North Pole, 'all the windows face south' —or almost all. Orbost, of course, has a ghost, and rather a curious one for the Hebrides, for it is the ghost of a coach and six, which is heard but never seen. It drives up to the front door not infrequently, with considerable noise and rattle and champing of bits, stamping of hoofs, &c., but everyone does not hear it. I have been in a room with four others; three of us heard it loud and clear, two could hear nothing. One of those who heard it did not know of the ghost at the time. Of late, however, it has been mechanized, which is most upsetting. Now it is a powerful car or lorry which drives up: the brakes are applied, later the clutch is let in and gears and acceleration can be heard as it departs. Only one sound we *never* hear; the door of car or coach is never opened or shut. What the story behind the coach and six was I never heard. Either my mother never knew or did not wish to frighten me as a child. But the coming of the coach could not be hidden.

Orbost must have been one of the last places where peafowl were regarded as a normal part of the poultry yard and roast peacock, or better still peahen, was an ordinary dish. Their habit of crying out before rain, however, makes them a doubtful blessing in the West.

The road passes behind the house and runs along the hillside above the sea as far as the sandy bay of Varkasaig,

once described as 'the white sands of Varkasaig'. The sands
turned black, as they now are, in a single night of storm.
The road is lovely (except to a car driver!) at all seasons:
primroses and bluebells are followed by honeysuckle and
roses, then comes the mass of blossom of a west coast July;
hardhead and scabious, orchis and pansy, meadowsweet
and asphodel, carpets of eyebright and milkwort and
thyme, and later heather, nuts, and rowanberries.

Again and again one longs for an authoritative book on
Skye place-names. Orbost and Varkasaig are both said to
be Scandinavian, Orbost being 'the homestead of the seals',
of which a great number once haunted the bay (there are
seal nurseries not far off), and Varkasaig being 'the place
of the great jumping beast', though this, I fear, is too good
to be true. This refers to an 'Each Uisge' or water-horse
which lives in the stream. At one time there was a shieling
not far from the burn and here an old woman and her
daughter came one summer to herd the cows. One night
there was a great storm of thunder, lightning, and rain.
When the storm was at its height there came a knocking at
the door of the shieling: the girl hastened to open it and
found on the threshold a very handsome young man, well
dressed but dripping wet, who begged for shelter. Rather
thrilled, the girl invited him in and offered him a place by
the fire and some oatcake and crowdie. He accepted both,
then settled himself near the maiden with his head on her
lap, where she sang him to sleep. When he slept the old
woman handed her a comb and, very gently, she began to
comb his hair. As the wise woman expected, it was full of
sand and small shells. Then they knew him for what he
was—a water-horse. The frightened girl gently moved his
head on to a bundle of unspun wool her mother brought
her, and slipped out of the house to cross the burn, knowing

that no supernatural creature can pursue across running water. But the hut was some way from the burn side and in a few moments the young man awoke: when he realized what had happened he at once reassumed his horse's shape and, roaring with fury, pursued the maiden in great leaps and jumps. Her mother was beforehand with him, however, and threw a naked knife in his path. As he paused she came up with him and said: 'If you pursue the cailin I will cry your name to the four brown boundaries of the earth', and she whispered his name. What it was or how she knew it has never been told, but the effect was instantaneous; with a terrible shriek the water-horse rushed to the burnside, plunged into the deep pool by the bridge, and vanished. It is said that, ignorant that the old woman has long since died, he has never again dared to venture far from his burn lest she name him, but those who go quietly on a fine summer evening may perchance see him frolicking all alone on the sand at the river mouth; and colts born in the valley exceed all others in strength and swiftness. But others say that the 'Each Uisge' made a pact with the wise woman, that every tenth year the burn should bring him a living sacrifice so long as he remained beneath its waters. If so, the Varkasaig river might, in its smaller way, vie with the Dee and the Don.

> *Bloodthirsty Dee*
> *Each year needs three;*
> *But bonny Don*
> *She needs but one.*

However, the kelpie seems to be content nowadays with an occasional rabbit.

Today anyone standing on the little bridge across the Varkasaig burn can see, up the valley and on the slopes and on Forse Park beyond, the signs of old cultivation. The hollows left by old drainage schemes and the old plough-furrows can still be clearly seen; so can the ruins of the 'old house' of Orbost among a few surviving trees in the valley. For once Orbost supported a fairly large population and the township of Orbost was not a small one. Its name was known far beyond the Islands and the reason for this was its school. There were, of course, no free government schools in those days and few of any variety in the Islands, but Orbost School, under the mastership of John Macpherson, grandson of that famous Rev. Martin Macpherson on whose account the Clanranald of the day was excommunicated, was famous throughout the North, and boys educated there became ministers of well-known churches in Edinburgh and Glasgow. Perhaps the most famous pupil of Orbost School was Donald Roy Macdonald, one of the Prince's guides. The Latin odes he wrote to pass the time when, wounded in the foot and with a price on his head, he lay hidden in a cave, are still extant and are said to be most scholarly.

Then came the Clearances. Of the how or why I can find no record. Was it by order of a proprietor who wanted sheep, or by the officiousness of a greedy factor, or by force of famine? All we know is that in about 1720 Orbost was a fair-sized township with a notable school but that when the property was sold to Miss Isabella Macleod's trustees in 1854 there was no township on the ground at all. The people of Orbost went as a community to Australia and there they founded a new township, now the large and flourishing agricultural centre of Orbost, Victoria, on the Snowy river. It looks a most attractive town on its postcards and 'folders', and curiously enough the photographer who took the photographs reproduced on them came from

Armadale, Victoria, which is, as it should be, near Broadford.

From Varkasaig a footpath climbs up over Forse Park, at first following the cliff top, then, near the Forse Burn, turning a little inland. The way to the Maidens is a most beautiful walk over short, springy turf smelling of thyme; over heather, across Forse Burn with its gorge, and through the two lovely valleys of Brandersaig and Idrigall until, at length, the end of the world seems to have been reached, with Macleod's Maidens seated in the sea below and beyond them the little skerries which are seal nurseries.

The views, changing all the way, are almost unbelievably beautiful: Loch Bracadale, that 'loch of many enchantments', with its panorama of islands coming into view one by one, first Rhum and Canna and Harlosh Island, then Tarner Island, Wiay, Eigg, and Muck, has a beauty no words can convey. And for those who like it, there is the old saw about the man who was 'born in Eigg, lived on Rhum, and was buried in Muck', but 'I Canna believe it'.

On the rocks below are fascinating pools filled with all ordinary and many rare pool folk: of sea anemones alone there are at least nineteen different colours and kinds on the Orbost rocks. Also, at the cliff's foot and to be visited only by boat, is the great Archway Cave of Idrigall with its fine natural arches, where the tragic Lady Grange was once imprisoned (see Chapter 10). These cliffs have seen much history—Viking ships and Irish coracles, men of war and men of peace, Stone Age burials of which a tradition still lingers, and perhaps men of the Firbolg. Over the loch below them strode Cuchullin, through it swam Col, holding fast to one of the bristles of the Golden Bristled Sow when she came from Ireland, bringing in her wake nine piglets and much misfortune. The Scone stone and the wild swans have blessed these waters. Here came ships of the Spanish Armada, and here one remained on the rocks. Here came a U-boat in the First World War to land prisoners: the only Germans to land freely on Britain's soil. And here Boswell caught a cuddy.

In the olden days, when the constant war between Macleods and Macdonalds was still a going concern, the Macdonald of the period and the Macleod of the period made peace together for a time, and Macdonald came to visit Macleod at Dunvegan. Now in those days it was customary for the chief to sit in judgement in his hall on any quarrel or dispute which his clansmen brought before him. While Macdonald was his guest just such a dispute arose. A certain Macleod was in the habit of grazing his cows on the moor between Forse and Idrigall, as he had the right to do. Another Macleod, a fisherman, usually kept his boat tied up in a sheltered opening in the rocks below the cliffs of Forse, as he was entitled to do. One night one of the cows, grazing on the cliff top, stepped too near the edge and fell over the cliff. The tide was high and had she fallen into the water she might have swum ashore unhurt, but she fell into the boat, smashed it to matchwood, and broke her neck. Thereupon the owner of the cow claimed compensation from the owner of the boat, on the ground that the boat had killed his cow, while the owner of the boat claimed compensation from the owner of the cow, on the ground that the cow had smashed his boat. Friends and neighbours joined in the quarrel and feeling at last ran so high that Macleod feared the clan might split in two over the matter. By now, personal pride was involved and a mere offer of compensation to both would not help. Then he had a brainwave. He would ask the old Macdonald chief to show that wisdom for which he was noted by judging this dispute: it would be a tactful compliment to his guest and, however he decided, Macleod himself could not be accused of taking sides. Macdonald expressed willingness and the trial began.

First the owner of the cow stated his case: but for the presence of the boat his cow would be alive and well. Then the owner of the boat had his say: the cow should have been tethered; but for it, his boat would be safe. There was a long silence. One or two among the crowd that had gathered in the hall whispered that the old chief dozed. Suddenly he opened his eyes and gave judgement.

'If the cow had not fallen over the cliff the boat would not have been harmed.' The owner of the boat began to look happy. 'If the boat had not been tied up at the cliff foot the cow might not have been harmed.' The cow's owner pricked up his ears. 'The fault therefore lies with the cliff. If the cliff had not been there, the cow could not have fallen over it. If the cow had not fallen over the cliff, both boat and cow would be unharmed. Who owns the cliff?' 'Macleod! Macleod!' answered a dozen voices. 'Then I judge Macleod must pay for both cow and boat' said the old chief, and amid deafening cheers, led by a much relieved Macleod, he dozed off again.

The Maidens themselves are three great rocks rising up out of the sea, a mother and her two daughters. At their feet the mermaids sit and comb their hair: very few see them but many hear their soft, unforgettable singing. Once a man lay long on the cliff top, watching the kites circling overhead and listening to the hum of the bees. Slowly the hum changed to a mermaid's song and he looked down and saw a mermaid and three seals on the rocks below. Somehow he got down the cliff unseen and caught, not the mermaid but one seal, a half-grown calf; as he held it the water round him boiled as with fish and out of it rose the heads of many mermaids. The one whom he had seen on the rocks still had her comb in her hand. She called to him and bade him release the baby seal and she would reward him. He agreed and asked for her golden comb as a reward. This she refused, but offered him instead three wishes, which offer he accepted but got no good of the wishes. One never does.

The largest of the Maidens, in shape and general appearance, is not unlike the statues of Queen Victoria seated when seen from the sea. She is the Mother (Nic Cleosgeir Mhor) and is said to be perpetually weaving, while one daughter fulls or thickens and the other does nothing at all. Perhaps they are shadows of the old Norse Fates, the Nornir, two of whom spun the threads which are the lives of men, but the third did nothing except cut them when she chose, for she is blind.

Sir Walter Scott called these rocks 'The Choosers of the Slain' and 'Riders of the Storm'. There was little he missed, and so perhaps he knew the old story (told in other Scandinavian parts of Scotland also) of the last appearance of the Valkyries, or Choosers of the Slain, over this very wing of Skye before they fled, conquered by the coming of Christianity.

It was their custom, before a battle, to weave the web of death, then choose the best and bravest of the slain and lead them to Valhalla where, in its hall with 540 doors, they feast on the great boar Sachrimner (which is whole again each morning) and other things, and tell tales of prowess in arms until Odin shall summon them to his side for the last and greatest battle of all.

One night—it was the eve of that Good Friday upon which the Battle of Clontarff was fought in 1014—a farmer who had been on the cliff top in search of a strayed beast

found all the world suddenly dark and, looking up for the
cause of the shadow, saw the twelve Valkyries hovering on
their swans' wings over Healaval. They were weaving their
dreadful web of death upon a loom of lances and the
weights of the loom were men's heads. As they wove they
sang (the translation by Gray is of a Caithness version of
their song):

> *Horror covers all the heath*
> *Clouds of carnage block the sun;*
> *Sisters, weave the web of death,*
> *Sisters, cease, the work is done.*

The song ceased and the farmer saw the Valkyries tear the
web into two pieces and fly off with them, one half to the
north, one half to the south, 'denoting the rending of
the ancient faith'. There is no record of the Valkyries being
ever seen again in Skye.

Some say the chief Maiden is Ran, wife of the Norse god-
ling or Vanir called Hler or Ygg or Oegir. It was Oegir's
custom to lift his hoary head from the waves when about
to call up a storm, to the undoing of ships. When she saw
this sign his wife, Ran, made ready and sat fishing for
sailors, whose spirits she imprisoned, until for her evil
practices she and her maidens were themselves imprisoned
in these stones. But they are neither dead nor helpless, for
always Macleod's Maidens have been known to contain
evil spirits who are wreckers of ships and drowners of men.
Perhaps they were helped in this by the noted wrecker and
smuggler Campbell of Ensor, who used the 'Black Skerries'
at the Maidens' feet for his false lights. Their ill reputation
began at least as long ago as John, fourth chief of Macleod,
a man of violent temper who made many enemies. After a
visit to Harris he was about to step into his galley when he

was stabbed to death. In the resulting confusion the galley, in which his wife and daughters had already taken their places, was swept out to sea without men or oars and finally drifted on to Idrigall Point by the Maidens, with the loss of all on board.

As late as in the last war a ship went ashore on the rocks near them. The captain and crew maintained that they were blown ashore by a gale helped by fast-running and strong currents setting on to the Point. But others said that such wind as there was was offshore and that no currents set that way.

The Maidens, excited perhaps by the war, had claimed another victim.

15

Roag, Harlosh, Bracadale

Two views of the barnacle:

When Calum na Croige returned from his week's swim he said the loveliest music he ever heard was that made by the barnacle geese as they emerged from the barnacles that had grown on the soles of his feet.

(From Campbell's *Superstitions of the Highlands and Islands of Scotland*)

A barnacle may be said to be a crustacean fixed by its head and kicking the food into its mouth with its legs.

(Huxley, *Encyclopaedia Britannica*)

THE road to Roag, when it turns off the Varkasaig road through the 'hole in the wall', dips down to cross the Orbost burn. Fifty years ago the banks of this burn were a vipers' breeding-place and snakes were so numerous about it that on a sunny day one might meet several in a few yards. Vipers are supposed to return year after year to the same nursery, but now there seem to be none at all on Orbost. Have they at last been exterminated? Vipers in the old days at Orbost, and indeed all over Skye, were something of a problem, as dogs and sheep were often bitten; so, sometimes, were the children running barefoot to school. Children and dogs could be cured, but among sheep the snake-bite 'black loss' was heavy. My father had a setter bitten on one occasion and the keeper cured it by bathing the injured paw in hot water containing a 'snake stone'.

A snake stone was rare and precious, to all appearances just a pebble with a hole through it, but vipers were believed to need these stones to crawl through and so slough off their old skins and, in return, gave to the stone certain virtues.

When my mother was a child she and her brothers were told, and firmly believed, that horse hairs floated in water would become eels and that these eels, in their turn, would leave the water and become snakes. Again and again they floated horse hairs hopefully in the millpond but were never lucky enough to see one turn, though the ultimate disappearance of the hairs and the quantity of vipers about proved conclusively that they did, and that frequently. Equally elusive in their habits were the barnacles which cover the Skye rocks: everyone knew that these in due course took wing and became barnacle geese, but the children, watch as they might, were never lucky enough to see one actually do it.

At the top of the hill beyond the burn there was once an old graveyard. All trace of it seems lost now except one: its ghosts still walk and few women, at any rate, like to pass alone there after dark. Beyond it lies a small hollow once known as Lag-an-t-Searrag, the Hollow of the Cup. Here there was a hollow stone used as a receptacle for milk poured out for the Gruagach which haunted the hollow. In old Gaelic 'Gruagach' meant a young chief, or more literally 'the long-haired one', but later it came to be used of a spirit, in some districts a long-haired youth in fine white shirt (often frilled) and knee-breeches, but more frequently in Skye the Gruagach was a very tall, thin woman with hair falling to her feet; she wore a soft, misty robe, the effect being described as like 'a white reflection or shade'. She was usually the former mistress of the house or land she haunted, who had either died in childbirth or been put under enchantment. She belonged to the site and not to the occupiers and she was seldom seen unless something was about to happen to that site. She helped the owners by caring for cattle and small children (so long as they allowed no dog near her) and the simple were under her protection. Like the English brownie, she was partial to a dish of cream. She could sometimes be heard or seen showing great joy or weeping. This reflected joy or sorrow about to fall on the house or land she served. The Gruagach of the Roag hollow seemed to have been forgotten entirely and her stone lost. But in 1920 two men were coming home along this road on a dark night when they saw on the moor not far off a clear, white light. At first they paid but little attention, feeling vaguely that it must be the moonrise. Then one of them realized that they were now in 'the dark of the moon' and there would be no moonlight. So they drew near and looked more carefully and they saw that the light came from two clear white figures in long shining robes who walked in the heather. The men said later that they felt no fear at the time, only awe and interest, for they knew that what they saw were no ghosts but intensely alive and, they added, 'shining and cold as hoar frost'. The men went on their way, neither hurrying nor loitering to watch: they were without power to choose, they said. For a time no one would go along the road after dark, and the township waited. Then the memory died, but a rather curious coincidence may have revived it. For some thirty years ago a man was found dead just at this point. As is usual, a cairn was raised to mark the spot and can still be seen. Two years ago an old man who lodged in a house near by was found dead on exactly the same spot. Their cairns are almost touching. He had been in bad health, but his sudden death was a surprise to all, and who could help asking: 'Why both on the same spot? And that spot so close to the old graveyard and the Hollow. Did they hear or see something? If so, of what did they die? Was it fear?'

A little farther on, Roag township proper begins, while a cart-track running down towards the sea links up the three Greep houses with the main road. Dr. Johnson is believed to have visited Greep's archway cave in the headland and Boswell to have caught his famous cuddy from those rocks.

Roag itself is most attractive, with glorious views of Loch Bracadale and the Cuchullins on one hand and Macleod's Tables on the other. One autumn day in 1263 the people of Roag looked out to see their loch full of ships, King Haco's defeated galleys, for after the Battle of Largs his fleet ran before the wind to Wester Fjord (Loch Bracadale), where his men landed and despoiled the countryside of all food, leaving starvation behind them. It is hardly to be wondered at that when, some years later, the Norsemen again attacked Skye and landed in Trotternish it was a Roag man, MacSween, who accepted the offer made by the Lord of the Isles to give the Braes to any man who would rid Skye of the invaders, or that he used somewhat doubtful measures to accomplish this end. The Battle of Blar-na-Buailte was fought on the shores of Score Bay in Trotternish and the invaders were defeated but not exterminated. One of their leaders, Arco Bronmhor, escaped with his following to the island in Loch Chaluim Chille, which they fortified, and proceeded to become a most active 'thorn in the flesh' to Skye. MacSween's assaults on the island were easily repulsed and matters seemed to have reached a deadlock when MacSween decided to try other and decidedly less chivalrous methods. He disguised himself as a bard and visited Arco. He was well received, as was becoming to one of that privileged class, and was admitted to the island, where he began, at Arco's request, to entertain him with songs and stories. A good dinner having preceded the entertainment, Arco soon fell asleep, whereupon his guest cut off his head (though why there were no guards is not related) and somehow succeeded in getting both it and himself away safely. He successfully carried the precious head to the Lord of the Isles and received in exchange the Braes of Trotternish and probably also much personal satisfaction.

The next fleet we hear of at Roag was that sent by the Earl of Argyll in 1558. Roag Pool must have been a heaven-sent anchorage in days of little ships, even if entrance and exit at high tide only would hardly suit an invader. However, the Campbells came on this occasion in peace, desiring to make some agreement on behalf of the Macleod heiress (so they said) with Iain Dubh, the usurping Macleod chief who had seized castle and lands by treacherously murder-ing various other members of his family. The Earl's emis-saries came to MacSween, Macleod's vassal in the Roag district, and asked him to arrange a meeting between them and his (temporary) chief. MacSween received them hos-pitably and arranged a meeting as they desired, to take place in the church of Kilmuir at Dunvegan. Iain Dubh re-ceived them in most friendly fashion, agreed to various suggestions, even seemed pleased by them, and then in-vited them to a banquet in the castle. Being lacking in sense (for was it not his reputation as a murderer which had brought them to Skye?) they accepted his invitation and were all duly murdered. Their servants escaped to Roag and, so forewarned, the main body of the Campbell host which was ashore there hastily put to sea once more and sailed for Argyll.

Roag has the distinction of being the first place in Skye

to 'serve a dish of tea'. A sailor visiting the East sent home a box of tea to his two old aunts, who shared a cottage in Roag. He mentioned that in his opinion tea was the most delicious thing that grew but omitted to mention whether it was delicious to eat or drink, also how to prepare it. The two old ladies had never heard of the Chinese 'Cha-king' or 'holy scripture of tea' in which the making is described, including the three stages of boiling water: 'the bubbles of the first boil should be as the eyes of fishes, the bubbles of the second boil as a fountain crowned with clustering crystal beads, and the final boil as a surge of miniature billows.' They decided to ask several neighbours in to share their treat and then put their heads together over how to serve it. If tea grows, they argued, it must be a vegetable, and accordingly they stewed the tea-leaves and served them with melted butter. They and their neighbours all politely agreed that the new vegetable was indeed delicious, but a desire for tea did not immediately become obvious in the district.

Another road branches off on the right to Ardroag and the shore. Those visiting the farthest house along this road at a very high tide must drive through the sea. Then comes the junction with the Dunvegan–Sligachan road, Dunvegan to the left and Sligachan to the right. Some two or three hundred yards in the Sligachan direction there takes off to the right the road through Vatten to Harlosh and Feorlig. At the corner is Vatten School and close to it one of the old 'earth houses' or 'Picts' houses' as they were more often called. Near Vatten is a spot called Bun a Sgamhaidh, or the 'Place of Refuse', which gets its name as follows. William Cleireach, or the Cleric, fifth chief of Macleod, was a younger son who inherited after the unfortunate death of his elder brother in a quarrel in Lewis. He had been destined for the Church but does not seem to have been particularly suited to such a peace-loving career, as his first act on becoming chief was to lead a large foraging party to the mainland and carry off all the Frasers' cattle from Easter Ross to avenge a slight he had received from them in his youth. The party returned to Skye with immense booty and proceeded to divide, kill, and cut up the herds at this spot: hence its name.

Harlosh is a peninsula with a youth hostel and some very beautiful views. The road runs down to the end, across and up the other side through Feorlig to rejoin the main Sligachan road, and the detour is well worth while. This peninsula must in the old days have been a very well-fortified area, as indeed were all Loch Bracadale's shores. Here we pass several duns, Dun Feorlig being probably the largest. The most interesting ancient monuments here, though, are the two big tumuli close to the point where the road from Harlosh rejoins the main road after passing through Feorlig. There are two traditions about these tumuli. One, very faint and now almost forgotten, tells how once in the long ago there was a very great chief: he owned all the land thereabouts and was 'Lord of every dun and of every galley'. Every summer he went to sea and returned with riches beyond men's dreams, gold and jewels, cattle, prisoners, and 'things not before seen'. One summer he did not return. The leaves had fallen and the moor was red before his fleet came slowly sailing home. His men landed, bearing on their shields the dead body of their chief. They dug a great grave, such as befitted a mighty chief, and in it they buried him and many of those who had slain him (alive or dead?). Every man laboured all day and for many days piling stones upon the grave. Then came a night when the Northern Lights played over his tomb and his men set fire to his galley drawn up on the beach, and sailed away to 'join the Merry Dancers'. But no stones, no ships burnt in appeasement, no slaves, could placate the 'Barrow Dweller', and the evil ghost still walks.

A later and much better-known tale tells of a battle here, 'the last ever fought between Macleods and Macdonalds'. MacCullough says 'it was fought in mist, like that last weird battle in the West'. So many were killed on both sides that none were left to bury the dead, so the old men and the women gathered them together, Macleods in one place and Macdonalds in the other, as they had stood to fight, and piled stones upon them; but their ghosts also walk.

Facts are harder to come by. There was in fact a battle at Feorlig early in the fifteenth century. Iain Borb (John the Truculent), sixth chief of Macleod, being a child and his tutor, Iain Mishealbach (John the Ill Fated) being, as his name implies, a good person to make war against, the Macdonalds thought it a tactful moment to seize both Castle Camus and Dun Scaith. Had they rested on their laurels all might have gone well for them, but instead they decided to attack Dunvegan Castle itself and were well and truly defeated at Feorlig by a mixed force of Skye and Uist men commanded by Macleod of Lewis in person, and *he* was not 'ill fated'. Though this battle was neither a great massacre nor the first or last fought by the rival clans, it may have given rise to the second of the tumuli stories.

When my mother was young these tumuli could be entered and she had been inside one of them some time between 1880 and 1890. There were, she said, several little rooms or cells off a passage, the centre one being the largest but none high enough for her (5 ft. 4 in.) to stand erect. The place felt dank and airless and she was glad to get out into the sunshine, whereas in one of the 'Picts' houses' she visited near Struan (probably Dun Beag) the atmosphere was entirely different, being fresh and warm as if the summer air percolated freely in spite of the absence of windows, and the dun was a pleasant place to visit or shelter in. This one had a passage right round inside the walls with low 'rooms' off it and a centre room or court. In one of the 'cells' were signs of recent occupation, including ashes. The duns were said to be sometimes visited by shepherds and gipsies in need of temporary shelter.

Bronze Age implements and jewellery were found, I believe, in the big tomb at Feorlig, but these have been lost. A big find of both Stone Age (Neolithic) and Bronze Age weapons was excavated from Dun Beag, however, and there seems little doubt that many, if not all, the duns go back to Neolithic times. Skye is exceptionally full of these prehistoric remains, particularly forts round the coast, and Loch Bracadale has more than its share of these last. There are two definite traditions about them, one of which makes them the dwellings of the Little People or of ghosts or spirits. There is danger in approaching them, especially after dark, and those mortals carried off by fairies were taken into the Duns, as were cattle or anything the Sithichean fancied, for the 'sitheins' were fairy homesteads or entrances, sometimes, to the fairies' country. This tradition asserts that they are 'as old as the Sithichean', meaning older than man. The stories which follow the second tradition are, as one might say, rationalized: the duns were forts built by the Danes and occupied by them when danger threatened.

Probably the first tradition is a faint and hazy memory of the original builders, Neolithic perhaps, driven underground by a conquering race but getting their own back

when they could. And then later, much later, comes a
memory of the use of the forts by later conquerors. Probably their 'building' by the Danes means in fact repairs by
the Norsemen, which may account for the number and
good condition of these strongholds here in historic times.

One of the largest and best preserved is that Dun Beag
already mentioned; it is in Struan, to the left of the road
just opposite the Ullinish turning. In 1770 its walls were
eighteen feet high and tradition doubles this at an earlier
date. Now the highest point is only twelve feet, less than the
thickness of the walls at the base. The fort is some 60 feet
in diameter. This dun has been partially excavated and
what appeared to be an armoury of late Stone Age weapons
was found, also certain Bronze Age relics and clear signs
of iron-working, yet tradition calls it a Viking fort.

Farther on, at the head of Loch Beag, is another dun,
Fort Gharsainn, at Totardair. Obviously this was once the
strong-point guarding a possible landing-place and in more
modern times it became renowned for the beautiful fairy
music which sometimes could be heard by those who
visited it, marking it out as a sithein of some importance.
For long all went well: then one day a young man who was
building himself a byre ran short of stone. He was of those
who have little use for fairies and he decided that the
stones of Gharsainn were worth some risk, but that his
neighbours might not see eye to eye with him in the matter.
He waited until nightfall, strapped two peat creels on his
horse, and went quietly to gather a stone harvest. Now it
so happened that all the fairies were away from the dun
that night: they had gone to help the Queen of Blaaven
to make a tartan suit for her son, who was to wed a king's
daughter, so for a little while the foolish boy worked in
peace and safely removed two loads of stone; but on the

third journey, when he put out his hand to touch the wall
an unearthly light shone out and voices warned him of the
vengeance of the Daoine Sithe and of evil things: he and
his horse turned and fled. The light was seen shining all
over the glen. Next day, some of the older people visited the
dun to see the cause and try, if needful, to appease the
anger of the fairies for the light had had a baleful quality.
When they reached the dun they saw an old man sitting
at the door of the fort, weeping and lamenting. At first he
did not seem to see them, but at last he replied to their
questions: 'I am weeping for the happy home that was. I
am weeping for the happy ones and the homestead to which
they will never return.'

After this he rose to his feet and making a sign in the
direction of the young man's house, incontinently vanished.
Then they knew they had talked to one of the Sithichean
and hurried from that place. But the fairies never returned,
their music and their singing were never heard again. As
for the young man, his horse died, his cattle sickened, his
crops failed, and his boat sank, and so at last he decided to
emigrate: whether or not the fairies' curse accompanied
him is not known. But there were those who blamed the
Bracadale Clearances on the malice of the evicted dwellers
of Dun Gharsainn.

Though these duns are near the road, we have gone too
fast. After the Harlosh and main roads join, the road continues down into the valley of the Caroy burn. Here are the
ruins of a little Episcopal church, the church of St. John
the Baptist, which stands in its own wooded churchyard
close to the sea. In late winter everything, even the
outlines of the graves, is hidden under a carpet of snowdrops. The church was built by the efforts of several Episcopalian families, said to have been led by Macleod of

Gesto. This was believed to be because 'Gesto' shot a seal on Sunday and was in consequence preached against in the old Church of Scotland church of St. Assynt at Struan (now a ruin) which his family had always attended, and in whose graveyard they are buried. This so annoyed him that he became an Episcopalian and did all he could to aid in the building of Caroy Church. Nevertheless, when his own time came he, too, was buried at Struan. Most of these families have long since disappeared and the little church, standing roofless, is a sad sight. For some reason Caroy graveyard is held to be very much haunted and by peculiarly powerful ghosts. 'Things' can be seen at night by the unwary also, though exactly what is never mentioned. They are not the ordinary churchyard ghosts, however, and the idea that the church was built and its graveyard laid out on the site of a prehistoric burial mound is very widespread. It was built on fairy ground, too, for beneath it the fairies used to 'waulk', or shrink, their cloth. Indeed, those who listen carefully at the appropriate season may still hear, faint and far away, the lilt of their waulking songs rising through the earth.

The sea has encroached considerably in the last 200 years and much once good grass-land at the head of Loch Caroy is now submerged. In 1745, when for the last time the fiery cross went round the Macleod lands in Skye, the place-name the runners shouted as they passed was 'Caroy', and here on the grass at the river mouth, now almost entirely sea-covered, gathered Clan Macleod in arms. Tradition says that of nearly 1,800 men who answered the summons believing that they were to fight for the Prince, only 500 remained when told that their chief had declared for King George. Of the remainder, some set off to join the Prince on their own and the rest returned quietly home.

Perhaps the chief was neither unduly surprised nor unduly disappointed at this result.

Passing Caroy Church the road runs on through the township of Ose with its sea-trout river and its lovely views, and over the hill beyond. Here a road takes off on the right to Ullinish, once honoured by a visit from Dr. Johnson and Boswell but now an hotel. Dr. Johnson stayed at Ullinish as the guest of Sheriff-Substitute Macleod and while there was shown all the sights of the neighbourhood: Dun Beag, of course, and also the three monoliths or standing-stones beyond the house. Local tradition has always maintained that they were erected 'long ago' for burning the dead and this tradition seems to be approximately correct, for a fairly recent find close to these stones was an ancient funerary urn full of ashes.

Another 'sight' was the little green hill near the house which, Boswell was told, was called the Hill of Strife because justice used to be administered here. Once there may have been families enough in Bracadale to keep the hill busy, but this is one of the areas from which many emigrated. The majority of the Evictions and forced emigration in Skye took place on the Macdonald lands while the estate was in the hands of trustees in the South, without knowledge of or sympathy with the tenants, and conceiving their only duty and interest to be the speedy settlement of various creditors and the freeing of the property from its difficult position, the outcome presumably of its forfeiture after the '15. But high rents and the terrible poverty brought about by the potato famine drove as hard as any evictors, and in 1830 a petition bearing the signatures of 300 Bracadale crofters was sent to London, petitioning for 'means to remove them to America'. Judging from the few who remain, means must have been found.

Not content with matters of interest on land near Ullinish, Johnson and Boswell put to sea and were taken to view the archway cave at Greep and also (indeed, this was the chief purpose of their trip) the Piper's Cave at Harlosh, but here they listened in vain for its echo. This is a cave of many entrances and in it an explorer may meet strange adventures. It connects with the Golden Cave at Dhubeag and Mac Coitir's Cave near Portree, with Fairyland, and, some say, with hell itself. In the local version of the Borreraig story (see Chapter 13) it was into this cave that the first of the great MacCrimmon pipers, as a young man, found his way and in it that he met a beautiful woman, believed to have been the Fairy Queen. He spent some time with her, feeling it but a few moments, and she asked him to tell her what parting gift he most desired: she presented him with his wish, a silver chanter, but she gave him also the gift to play it so that 'when you would dance all shall dance and when you lament the lamenting shall be on all the island'. But at a certain day and time he must promise to return to the cave and to her. This MacCrimmon, being under her spell, very readily undertook to do. He returned to Borreraig and became not only the greatest piper of his own day but the most famous there has ever been. He and his family were made hereditary pipers to Macleod of Macleod. In due course the day arrived on which he must keep his tryst with the Daoine Sithe. He said goodbye to his wife and family, for he knew full well he would never return, took his fairy chanter and set off for Harlosh, but before he left home he 'wished' his gift of music upon his son. MacCrimmon entered the cave playing his pipes, with his little terrier dog at his heels barking madly. His sons and others had accompanied him to the cave's mouth. They followed the sound of his pipes and the

barking of his dog, both of which could be clearly heard
beneath the moor, to a spot near Fairy Bridge: here the
sound of the pipes ceased but the barking could still be
heard, and this led them to Dhubaig. As they approached
the bay the barking grew clearer until at last out of the
Golden Cave ran the little terrier, with every hair singed off
his body!

Beyond the Ullinish turning the hill road to Portree
takes off to the left. This hill road is the most inland one in
Skye, it being possible at one spot to be as much as four
and a half miles from either coast. The main road winds on
through Bracadale and down a long hill into the township
of Struan. Here, by the Voaker burn, is a derelict church;
near it, in the same graveyard, the old parish church of St.
Assynt, patron saint of Bracadale, once stood. It was one
of the original Skye churches and served a large population.
In its churchyard, still in use, are some very old graves. At
this point the road turns inland along the shore of Loch
Beag.

16

Bracadale

*And the big hills up behind it, like the monarchs of
   the land,*
*Sitting throned above the waters, dreaming sadly,
   hand in hand,*
*And the sad sea, sighing, sobbing, throbbing, wailing
   o'er the strand,*
And the faces that I long for evermore.

('The Glen of Dreams' by Lauchlan Maclean Watt)

ABOVE Struan's scattered township there lies a small loch,
Loch Duagrich, in Glen Bracadale. Here there was once a
shieling in which nine girls were spending the summer
herding cows. One evening an old woman came to the
shieling and begged for a night's shelter, and the girls wel-
comed her and gave her a place in their big bed. One girl,
however, had the toothache, and woke to see her sucking
blood from the neck of the girl next her. Realizing that she
was a kelpie, the girl sprang from the bed and rushed out,
screaming, into the night with the kelpie in pursuit.
Frightened as she was, she kept her head and ran straight
for the Voaker burn: once across running water she was
safe. By the morning the old woman had vanished but the
other eight girls were all found lying dead in the big bed as
the kelpie had left them. Her toothache had saved the
ninth girl's life.

Naturally this terrible occurrence caused much nervous-
ness in the district and made everyone very wary with
strangers, with the result that the poor kelpie had great

difficulty in catching a human at all or getting enough to eat. So one day this same kelpie, taking the form of a young man, approached a cottage in Bracadale where the mistress of the house was busy making porridge for her children's dinner, and asked her who she was. She replied (being pretty sure who *he* was), 'Myself is Myself'. 'I never heard that name before', commented the kelpie, who was really rather a young and foolish one, 'I have come a long way and am very hungry; will you give me some of your porridge?' 'All of it, gladly', replied the woman, and emptied the pot over his head. He rushed home, screaming, to his parents, who angrily demanded who had burnt him. 'Myself, Myself', moaned the injured creature. 'Then we can do nothing, not even avenge you', lamented his parents. And apparently he never explained. It is curious to find such a well-known Greek story so far from Greece, and tempting to believe that its hero slipped quietly, not out of Loch Duagrich at all, but out of the pages of a book in use at Orbost School, where Greek was taught. Only, if so, how did the Golden Bristled Sow get out of the Welsh Triads into Loch Bracadale, or the white cattle of the Welsh lake fairies come to Gesto, when the Highland fairy cattle are usually brindled?

The road winds on round the head of Loch Beag and up the long and steep hill beyond it, with beautiful views of sea and mountains and of Talisker Head with its cliff. No wonder it was Cuchullin's stepping-stone.

At almost the highest point another road takes off to the right: this is the road to Gesto, one of the oldest houses, as opposed to castles, in the island, but it has fallen upon evil days and is now a ruin. Perhaps the reason for that may be this very road, for it is one of the worst hills in Skye. Once the woods through which it ran were carpeted with snowdrops, but now the sheep have destroyed them, like so much else. The house itself stands almost on the sea-shore, in a very sheltered little bay, and, what is most unusual in Skye, in its own garden. The first slated house in Skye, slated properly with heather nails. Gesto must once have been a most charming dwelling.and, unlike most Skye houses, it was covered with flowering creepers, roses, and honeysuckle.

Murdo Macleod, third son of Malcolm the third chief of Dunvegan, was the first of Gesto. He married a daughter of Gillies of Glen Suardale, 'a great warrior of Skye', and she brought him as her tocher or dowry Gesto 'and the length of Tubic in Tuick, and Ault in Carrick in Drynoch, and to the water of Skiairaig, between Struan and Belgorm on the other side'. In fact much land. And here begins the Gesto mystery, which has never, so far as I know, been satisfactorily solved.

As a cadet of the Macleods of Dunvegan, Macleod of Gesto owed fealty to his chief. But his lands were never Dunvegan lands and for them he owed neither service nor rent, nor did he pay either until, in 1674, without explanation he took a tack or lease of his own land of Gesto from the then Macleod of Macleod, and in 1825 Macleod refused to renew his tack and kept the property. Here is the mystery. How did Macleod of Macleod ever come to be in the position to lease or refuse to lease this land of Gesto? No one appears to know. Gesto family tradition has a story about the matter which tells how the lands of Gesto were declared forfeit by Macleod of Macleod to Macleod of Macleod during the reign of James VI. There are, however, three versions of what occurred.

All three versions agree that three young men, 'Gesto' himself, his brother-in-law MacAskell of Ebost, and Macleod of Macleod's heir, were drinking and gaming together, but from there on they differ. The Gesto version is that a quarrel broke out, 'Gesto' resenting a slighting reference to his wife by MacAskell. Both grew heated and finally 'Gesto' challenged MacAskell to a duel and asked young Macleod to act for both. This was agreed to and 'Gesto' killed his man. Then Macleod took a hand and gave him a choice: he would tell what had occurred and clear 'Gesto' of a possible murder charge, he said, only if 'Gesto' would agree to accept a tack of his lands in future in place of ownership. It could be explained that he had staked it at cards and lost. If he would not do this, then Macleod would deny the duel and let him be tried for murder. 'Gesto' refused and was in fact found guilty of murder by Macleod of Macleod and sentenced to the forfeiture of his estate which had for more than 200 years been the only land in northern Skye not under the control of Dunvegan, though, tradition has it, not unnaturally coveted by them.

The Dunvegan version is simple. 'Gesto' having treacherously murdered his brother-in-law, he was declared forfeited of his estate.

There was, however, a third version, that of MacAskell's servant who had been in attendance on his master on the fatal night and an eye-witness of what had occurred. His story was that all the young men had been drinking heavily before the quarrel broke out. He did not hear (most tactful, that!) the remark which caused it but did hear 'Gesto' challenge his master to a duel. He helped to clear the room. Early in the fight his master caught his sword in a rafter (the room in Gesto in which the duel was traditionally fought was only seven feet high) and while thus disarmed was stabbed by 'Gesto'. He thought that 'Gesto' tried to stop when he saw MacAskell defenceless but was not in a 'sufficiently alert humour' to do so. He thought young Macleod tried to knock up Gesto's blade but he, too, was not sufficiently alert. In fact, he either believed that 'Gesto' 'murdered' MacAskell but accidentally in a duel, or else he was engaged in a very clever avoidance of disagreeing either with his chief's son who said 'murder' or his mistress's brother who said 'duel'. So far as is known, no notice was ever taken of his testimony.

'Gesto' fled for sanctuary to his wife's father at Cuidrach, and the story goes that when the MacAskells came there for him they found 'Old Cuidrach' on guard, sword in hand, and preferred returning unaccompanied to attempting to remove a guest from the house of Do'ull MacIain 'ic Sheamuis, who was still the most noted swordsman of his day in the North, despite his grey hairs.

Though all agree that Gesto was forfeited, so far as is known nothing happened, and Macleod of Gesto continued to live there peacefully, once the first excitement was over, while his wife and family never left it, just as Rory Mor, chief of Dunvegan, when all his lands were declared forfeit to the Crown about this time, and actually given to the Company of Gentleman Adventurers, continued to reside at Dunvegan quite unperturbed, and appeared no whit the worse for the forfeiture.

It is possible, however, that some unrecorded compromise was reached and that 'Gesto' did have to give up some portions of the estate while retaining Gesto proper, or that he did surrender his land to Rory Mor and receive it back as a tack. But if so, there is no record of the new relationship before 1674 and Sir Rory Mor died in 1626. When the change did come it was accompanied by considerable bitter feeling, ending in a lawsuit about boundaries in the time of the twenty-first chief. Neil Macleod won his case but this

time lost his estate in earnest, for Macleod of Macleod refused to renew his lease which expired in 1825, thus ending
almost 500 years of unbroken tenure. The property was
eventually sold to the Government for land settlement
after the First World War, and the ruined house and
grounds are now in the possession of a great-granddaughter
of the last Macleod of Gesto.

At the time of the actual forfeiture and for a time thereafter there seems to have been little or no friction between
Dunvegan and Gesto, Neil MacTormont (Macleod of Gesto)
and his son Murdo being named by Rory Mor in 1616 as two
of his principal clansmen who were to appear with him
before the Council in Edinburgh every year. There is, however, no evidence that they ever did so appear: the King's
writ sat very lightly on Skye in those days!

The old house knew many stories: there was that 'Gesto',
for instance, who refrained from marrying until he reached
the ripe age of forty-five and then set his affections on a
maiden of sixteen who did not see eye to eye with him at
all on the matter. But she was inordinately fond of butter;
so her mother, desiring the marriage, pointed out to her
that as mistress of Gesto she would also be mistress of its
dairy, and this had the desired result. To be mistress of
that particular dairy was no small thing in those days, for
the herd of pedigree Gesto cattle was a famous one. They
were pure white shaggy Highland cattle, large and with
magnificent horns just tipped with black. They were bred
at Gesto for several centuries and were descendants of a
fairy herd presented to Murdo Macleod about 1365 by the
Daoine Sithe.

Once this Murdo saw two of his men, who were engaged
in building him a new byre, destroying Dun Taimh near
Gesto by taking stones from it to use in the building. This

he forbade, explaining that at any moment the dun might
be needed as a refuge or stronghold and so they must take
stones from the shore instead. Now although 'Gesto' did not
know it, this dun was a Sithein (fairy dwelling) and the
Daoine Sithe, not hearing his reason for sparing their walls,
seeing only that he had saved them, were grateful. That
night he received a message bidding him come to the little
green knoll by the sea (now the boathouse hill). He kept
the tryst and found himself among a crowd of fairies,
young and old. An old fairy made him a speech of gratitude
'in the grand manner' and then proposed to toast his
health. The toast was enthusiastically honoured by the
company but with profuse apologies for not offering him
food and wine also, but if he touched their food he could
not return to earth for one year, they told him, and if he
drank their wine he would lose his soul. They then explained that their intention in inviting him to meet them
was to reward him. He had 'built him a byre from the
stones that harmed none'; they would fill it. And the old
man called out of the sea a herd of fifty perfect snow-white
cattle. 'These and theirs', said he, 'shall serve thee and
thine for 500 years.' Then the fairy company vanished and
the cows, lowing gently, made for the new byre.

As a child I saw what was, I believe, the last of the pure
Gesto bulls left in Skye. It was at Tote. He was a most
beautiful creature and had just returned (in a thoroughly
bad temper) from a prize-winning visit to a mainland show.
But the cows were said to be gentle and exceptionally good
milkers for cows of Highland blood. There are none left in
Skye today. The last of the pure herd known were in Argyll,
I was told, at Barguillian, and there may be some there
still, but of course the 500 years are now up!

After this, cattle became, as may be supposed, a great

Gesto interest and it seems only suitable that it should
have been the birthplace of what was to prove Skye's chief
industry for over 200 years, the breeding of little black
cattle for the southern markets. But it was not begun or
planned by a 'Gesto'. The 'Gesto' of the day (the reign of
James VI) was both scandalized and disapproving. The
matter arose in this way. John Macleod of Gesto married
Mary, daughter of Macdonald of Kingsburgh, better known
as Do'ull MacIain 'ic Sheamuis, the famous warrior and
hero of the Battle of Coire na Creiche. Later in life he came
for a time to live with his daughter and son-in-law and
while there he took up cattle-breeding on a large scale and
himself drove his herds to markets as far south as Falkirk
and Crieff. That he should so demean himself caused great
annoyance to his relatives and specially to his son-in-law,
'Gesto'. In fact it was considered such a crying scandal that
at last it reached the King's court in Edinburgh. When
King James heard it he is reputed to have said: 'I have in
Scotland a thousand men daring enough to drive cattle
from the south to the north (cattle lifting) but only one, it
seems, with courage to drive the northern cattle south
again.' And indeed Do'ull MacIain 'ic Sheamuis's worst
enemies admitted that it was a feat.

Fighting in one way or another was always a favourite
'Gesto' occupation, however. Probably the best known was
Lieutenant-General Norman Macleod of the Royal Nether-
lands Army, with his nine orders and decorations. He
joined as a cadet at the great age of eleven and served for
fifty-six years.

But to return to the butter-loving bride: besides butter
the child loved dolls and took one with her to her new
home. Her husband was not only older than herself but
very serious-minded, not to say fussy, and after their first

baby arrived he was much worried by her casual attitude towards it. One day, when approaching the house he looked up and saw his wife sitting at the low open window of the drawing-room, which was on the first floor as was then the custom, dandling the child on her knee. 'Be careful', he called anxiously. 'Don't sit so near the window. The baby might fall. Go in. It's very dangerous.' 'Catch!' replied his exasperated wife, and threw him the child. Somehow the terrified (and furious) father caught the bundle of shawls and laces; out of it peered the face of his wife's doll.

The next event of interest occurred between the two Risings, the '15 and the '45. This was the beginning of a number of mysterious disappearances which led in the end to the discovery of a great scandal. It might be a girl who had gone out to gather dulse on the rocks or a young man late on the hill who disappeared and was never seen again, but the number grew until few dared walk alone. At last the disappearances came to Gesto. A young girl was weaving some crotal-dyed tweed for her lover and the web was almost finished when she ran out of crotal. It was a Sunday, but in spite of her mother's protests she went down to the shore at Gesto to gather crotal (a yellow lichen) off the rocks there to finish her work, at an hour when all the glen was in church, and she was never seen again. In vain her people searched for her; the sea or the Evil One had taken her and, as is well known, the bodies of those who wear or hold crotal are never found. The tale was considered a moral one: evils befall those who disobey their parents or profane the Sabbath. It was therefore spread abroad; it can now be read as one of the Kennedy Fraser songs. But 'Gesto' himself did not believe the tale as told; he maintained that in his opinion those who strayed from the straight and narrow path were helped, not hindered, by the Devil! And he started inquiries which were most unpopular in some quarters. However, before he could learn much the whole racket was blown sky-high. A ship was wrecked off the coast of Antrim and enough survivors reached the shore to prove beyond doubt that one Norman Macleod of Unish, son of Macleod of Bernera, was doing an excellent trade by carrying off young men and girls, shipping them to America, and there selling them as slaves. The trade was stopped, 'Unish' protesting that he was really a most virtuous person who only shipped off known thieves and ex-convicts, but no serious effort seems ever to have been made either to trace and buy back the unfortunate victims or to punish their abductor. Accusations that he was backed by people in high places were not lacking but were never proved. It is on record that a Skye man in Canada lost his way and stopped at a lonely farmhouse to ask where he was. A girl came to the door and he spoke to her in English but she did not respond; he tried French and then German without success; then, almost unthinkingly, he exclaimed in Gaelic: 'Is there no language you will be speaking?' Instantly the girl broke out into a flood of words and told him how she had been carried off from Skye a few months previously by Norman Macleod and sold in America. She said she was well treated but very homesick and inquired eagerly for news of her family; she was always believed to have been the crotal gatherer.

After the Gesto turning the main road approaches the Cuchullins and with every mile the view of the mountains grows finer. Soon Loch Harport opens out to the right, and on the left waterfalls foam down the mountainside in white cascades, close by a road with some most alarming hairpin bends. At the head of Loch Harport a road takes off on the right hand and runs steeply downhill to cross the Drynoch river close to the head of the loch. Here are Drynoch Lodge and the site of the old house. Beyond it the road forks, that to the right leading to Carbost, with its 'Talisker Distillery', Ferrinlea, where Dr. Johnson landed on his way to visit Macleod of Talisker, then on to Portnalong, with its government settlement of Harris weavers. It would be interesting to know whether these are still looked on with the same dislike and jealousy as was once felt for their forefathers when they invaded Skye, or, indeed, for the weavers themselves when their advent was first planned. 'Just a lot of Harris thieves', says Skye of Harris. What Harris replies it is better only guessing!

The left-hand fork leads to Talisker itself and to Eynort.

Loch Eynort and the glens of Drynoch and Sligachan were the scene of one of the earliest and fiercest battles between Macdonalds and Macleods. The Battle of Loch Sligachan was in 1375. The Lord of the Isles of that day, having disinherited his family by his first wife in favour of the sons of his second, gave Skye, over which he and others claimed overlordship, to one of his first wife's sons, Ranald, ancestor of Clan Ranald, as recompense, and sent his brother Alasdair Carach with a large force to seize the island from the Macleods. The MacAskell of the day, Warden of Dunscaith and hereditary coast-watcher for Macleod, was caught napping, so the Macdonalds landed unopposed in Loch Eynort and marched up the Drynoch valley, laying all waste in their passage. At the head of Loch Sligachan, however, they were met by the Macleods in force and, after a struggle, retreated to their ships, pursued by the Macleods. MacAskell, anxious to atone for his carelessness, had meanwhile seized the Macdonald galleys and anchored them at some distance from the shore. The Macdonalds, finding themselves cut off, were thrown into confusion and suffered heavily. Skye tradition says that the Macdonalds were having the best of the battle when Tormod Coil Macleod of Gesto, a cousin of the chief, killed Alasdair Carach, cut off his head, and held it up. This turned the tide. On reaching the shore most of the Macdonalds were done to death and their heads cut off, counted, and sent to the Warden of Dunvegan for safe custody. Unfortunately for tradition, Alasdair Carach is known to have been still alive in 1411, when his estates were forfeited for his share in the insurrection of Donald Balloch. However, victory must have favoured the Macleods for they continued to hold Skye.

Many centuries later a Macleod shepherd, watching his sheep on the slopes above Loch Eynort, saw the graves in the old burial-ground there open; out of them rose a host of Macleod warriors, slain in this battle, perhaps. As they passed over him they lifted him up among them, and so held he flew through the air with these spirits of his ancestors over the sea to Harris. On the way they called at each graveyard in turn and at each were joined by Macleod ghosts, Trumpan in Waternish being the last place of call. In the air over Harris they met with a huge flight of Macdonald spirits, also carrying a mortal. The two humans, Macdonald and Macleod, were set down on the machair (sea-grass plain) to fight one another while the ghostly clans stood guard. All night they fought, to the joy of the ghosts, but by dawn no harm was done and each man was then lifted and carried back whence he came. On the return journey again each graveyard in turn was visited, this time Trumpan being the first and that on Loch Eynort the last. The fight, said Macleod, took time, for the fighters were mortal, but on the flight there was no time at all.

Macleod's Maidens, Loch Bracadale

The Natural Archway, Loch Bracadale

Near this same burial-ground there was once a small chapel dedicated to St. Maelrhuba, patron saint of Bracadale. Like all old Skye churches, it has become a ruin; but on one night of storm towards the end of the nineteenth century a fishing-boat from south Uist found itself in danger and ran for shelter to Loch Eynort. The fishermen landed and went up to the little ruined church to return thanks for their safety and to pray for good weather. There they found the old stone font with its beautiful antique carvings. They were Roman Catholics and thought it sacrilege to leave a consecrated font exposed to the weather, and, still worse, in Protestant hands, so they carried it carefully on board their boat and, the gale having dropped, put to sea. But at once the wind rose again, mountainous waves pounded the boat, and back to Loch Eynort they ran. Again the storm dropped, again they put to sea, again the wind rose and drove them back. This time it occurred to them that perhaps St. Maelrhuba wanted his font and did not wish them to remove it, so they returned it to the ruins and had a calm and pleasant voyage to Glasgow, their destination. But the font worried them. On the return journey they again called at Loch Eynort. This time they went ashore and prayed to St. Maelrhuba for a sign. Did he, they asked, wish them to carry his font to south Uist as a gift to their priest and for its proper use, or to leave it in the ruins? The sun came out, a favouring breeze arose, and the fishermen took heart again and, lifting the font with great reverence, carried it once more on board their boat. This time the weather favoured them and the font was soon safely in the hands of their priest. After his death his successor gave it to the Celtic antiquarian, Mr. Carmichael, and he presented it to the Society of Antiquaries in Edinburgh, in whose museum it now rests in peace.

Before the Carbost and Talisker fork a road turns sharply back and goes farther afield, through Glenbrittle, famous for its views of the Cuchullins at whose feet it lies, to the shores of Loch Brittle. In the pre-war days Skye had an airfield here and not only ambulance planes but a regular air-service, but the road became so bad that not even ambulance planes or 'mercy planes' now visit Skye, their place having been taken by a large Government forestry scheme.

But to return to the main road to Sligachan. Not far from the Drynoch corner as the crow flies, near the entrance to Loch Harport, is Rudha nan Clach, the Point of Stones; these are some old Druidical stones near the cliff edge. It is said that when the Cailleach Bhur (see Chapter 3) sprang from a mountain in Duirinish (believed by some to be Healaval Beg) to Ben Cruachan in Argyll to escape from the wrath of the sun, she touched these stones with her foot, and that is why there is a point of the same name in Mull, where the 'Shrieking Hag', as they called her there, landed when she came to Mull to die after a life of many thousands of years. A lament for her death was sung there into modern times.

From here on, the road to Sligachan runs through a large valley beneath the shadow of the Black Cuchullins. It is a fertile glen, though now lonely beyond words, with only the sheep for company. In the thirteenth century it was much fought over; later it became the site of a large and flourishing township. It is said that the district of Skye on the Hunter river in Australia owes its name to the emigrants from this part of the island. Let us part from them with the version from Kenneth Macleod's 'Road to the Isles' of the old Blessing on those who travel far:

May the hills lie low,
May the sloughs fill up,
    In thy way.

May all evil sleep,
May all good awake,
    In thy way.

SOUTH SKYE

Lament of Ossian in his old age

And long for me is each hour new-born,
Stricken, forlorn, and smit with grief
For the hunting lands and the Fenian bands,
And the long-haired, generous Fenian chief.

I hear no music, I find no feast,
I slay no beast from a bounding steed,
I bestow no gold, I am poor and old,
I am sick and cold, without wine or mead.

(Translated by Dr. Douglas Hyde from *The Book of the Dean of Lismore*)

17

Kylerhea

———•■•———

*Fionn, King of the Fenians, the generous one, was
without blemish! All the qualities which you and
your clerics say are according to the rule of the
King of the Stars, Fionn's Fenians had them all,
and if they are in pain, great would be the shame,
for if God Himself would be in bonds, my Chief
would fight on his behalf. Fionn never suffered
anyone to be in pain or difficulty and can his
doom be in Hell, in the House of Cold?*

(Ossian's reply to St. Patrick's opinion that Fionn
would be in Hell, as recorded in 'Dialogues of the
Ancients', an eleventh-century compilation)

BEFORE the building of Dornie Bridge, opened in 1942,
the Glenelg–Kylerhea ferry was a very popular motoring
route to Skye as it involved only one ferry instead of two,
but now the road is little used. It is a most lovely, though
lonely, drive through the hills to Broadford. The first
time we came by it, having crossed the ferry and climbed
about a mile, we came to an obliterated notice-board. We
thought: 'That must have been a sheep notice', and left it
at that, driving on in our fairly big and heavy Wolseley.
Later we came to the second board, pointing, of course, in
the reverse direction, and out of curiosity stopped to read
it. It said: 'No Car Road. The Next Seven Bridges Unsafe
For Traffic.' I hasten to add that those bridges are now
safe.

However, that was nothing to the car-ferry at Kyleakin in its early days, when it consisted of two planks across a row-boat. On to those planks, with care and skill and at certain states of the tide only, the car must be driven; then it was made fast with ropes through the wheel spokes. If it was a calm day all was well, but if the centre of the kyle was choppy, and it often is choppy from the point of view of a rowing-boat, there came the awful moment for the car-owner when the ropes were cast off with the ominous words: 'If she (the boat) rolls too much now, she (the car) will just slip off and maybe not sink us.' Nevertheless, though it looked and sounded alarming I never saw a car 'slip off' and only heard of one being lost. The ferrymen knew their job well.

Although today most people, including the Queen, come to Skye by Kyle of Lochalsh, not one of Skye's historic or other famous visitors did so. Cuchullin took two strides from Ireland and landed on Talisker Head: Robert the Bruce and Sir Walter Scott came to Dunvegan: James V with his retinue landed at Portree, and to Portree came R. L. Stevenson also: St. Columba and Bonnie Prince Charlie preferred the shores of Loch Snizort: Haco, King of Norway, first set foot in Bracadale, it is claimed, *en route* for the Battle of Largs: Dr. Johnson and Boswell, and the Fiennes, chose to come by way of Glenelg but Johnson and Boswell, once there, took boat for Armadale, not Kylerhea.

The first famous people to use Kylerhea were the Fiennes. Glenelg and Kylerhea have always been their country. According to tradition they were a race of fair and powerful giants, great hunters and fighters; they were either pre-Celtic or Celtic and came to Scotland from Ireland, and to Skye from Glenelg, one of their chief strongholds. Their chief was Fionn. A. R. Forbes in his *Place Names of Skye* recounts how two large burial-mounds were found at Imir nam Fear Mora (Field of the Big Men) in Glenelg. These were believed to be the graves of Fiennes and to have been opened in the presence of the then Minister of Sleat, who bore witness that in them were found the bones of huge men, bigger than any alive at the time. The Fiennes defended the Highlands from the sea pirates. Their leader, Fionn, was not only a great warrior but had a 'tooth of wisdom' which, when pressed, would answer any question truly. The Fiennes seem to have had attached to them almost all the tales of magic made familiar to us in our childhood in the German version of the brothers Grimm but proved by the late Andrew Lang to have been widespread and similar over the whole Aryan-speaking world, from India to Scandinavia. Grimm's heroes, however, were usually most immoral people, murder and theft being highly thought of, but the Fiennes had a very different code, not unlike that credited to King Arthur and his knights.

Martin Martin, writing in Skye in 1716, says of Fionn himself that he was the Highlander's conception of a gentleman. He was 'a kind friend, an adviser of judgement, wise in counsel, able to solve doubts and difficulties, hospitable to all, ever ready to protect the weak or defenceless'. Two old Gaelic sayings, too, have come down to us. They are:

The door of Fionn is always open and the name of his Hall is the Stranger's Home;

and

None ever went sad from Fionn.

Fionn's dog was Bran, the fearless and wise; his sword was Mac an Luin, Son of Light, which could put to flight even 'the Black Nameless Thing', the 'Fear that walked in the Dark'.

Of the Fiennes Martin Martin writes:

A candidate must give security that no revenge will be attempted for his death: must compose at least one song: be a perfect master of his weapon, a good runner and fighter. He must be able to hold out his weapon by the smaller end without a tremble: in the chase through wood and plain his hair must remain tied up; if it fell he was rejected. He must be light and swift so as not to break a rotten branch by standing on it, he must leap a tree as high as his forehead and get under a tree no higher than his knee: without stopping he must be able to draw a thorn from his foot: he must not refuse a woman without a dowry, must offer violence to no woman; be charitable to the poor and weak, and he must never refuse to fight nine men of any other race should they set upon him.

To this has been added that no Fienne must go back upon his vow, though it cost him his life.

One of the Fiennes' most cherished possessions was the Cup of Lewes, or the Cup of Worth as it was more often called: this was a square jewelled cup with four sides and four handles. When he who was worthy drank from it, he could drink what he wished; from one side red wine, from the next white wine, from the third mead, and from the fourth pure spring water. But for the worthless man it would produce nothing. Some have connected it with the Dunvegan Cup, which also is square, jewelled, and ancient Irish.

The Fiennes dwelt near Glenelg in the duns on the river Allt Mor Ghalltair and used to hunt on Mam Rattachan; but deer grew scarce there so Fionn took to leading his men across the kyle into Skye on large-scale hunting expeditions, where they were in the habit of killing as many as 6,000 deer in a day, so it is said. Naturally these hunts had a bad effect on the island's food supplies, and as deer grew

scarcer the Fiennes grew hungrier and thinner, but their
wives, whom they left at home in Glenelg, became fairer
and fatter. This greatly annoyed Fionn, especially as his
wife Grainnhe and her ladies would not reveal their secret.
When next they went hunting, Fionn left Conan to watch
the women secretly. Thinking themselves unobserved they
gathered hazel tops, boiled and ate them, then washed
their faces in the juice. Conan, overcome by hunger, re-
vealed himself. Pretending no anger at his spying, the
women fed him and then, while he slept, tied his hair to a
hundred stakes and awoke him suddenly. Conan leaped to
his feet, leaving his scalp behind. This pleased the gentle
Grainnhe and her maidens but it did *not* please Conan, who
drove them into a hut, piled heather round it, and set it
alight. The Fiennes hunting in Skye saw the smoke and the
blaze; with long leaps they crossed the moorland, sword
in hand they leaped the strait. The women were saved but
Conan lost the rest of his head. Mac an Raeidhinn, one of
the Fiennes, fell short in his leap and was drowned in the
kyle, which ever since has been called Kylerhea after him.

As you drive down the road towards Broadford, three
peaks can be seen to the north; the first two are Beinn na
Greine (2,000 feet) and Scurr na Coinnich (2,401 feet); the
third and most northerly is Beinn na Caillich (2,396 feet).
This last must not be confused with the Beinn na Caillich
near Broadford which is one of the Red Cuchullins although, just to make it more confusing, on the summit of
our Beinn na Caillich, as on that of her larger sister, tradition has placed a woman's grave. This time it is that of a
giantess, one of the Fiennes: beneath her body is a large
crock filled with gold and jewels, for she was a great lady,
no less than Grainnhe herself, wife of Fionn, and at her
burial every man of the Fiennes, for love of her and of their

leader, cast their rarest jewels into the earthenware crock to do her honour. Her story, as is so usual in Celtic legend, is a sad one. Grainnhe is the daughter of the King of Morven and is reputed the fairest and truest princess in all Alban, so the Grey Magician, who hates all that is good, carries her off. One day, as Fionn and his men rest after hunting, an old, old woman, wrapped in the red mantle that denoted royal blood, comes to him, tells him of the theft of Grainnhe and begs him to rescue her. He agrees, whereupon she gives him a fir twig and three small pebbles, all highly magic; she then goes out of sight 'on an eddy of the western wind, growing smaller as she went until she seemed no bigger than a butterfly, a honey bee, a red spider on a thin rope of its web, and a speck of dust in the sun'. Fionn sets out and after many adventures, during which he is assisted by several talking animals, he finds the Grey Magician's palace and escapes with Grainnhe. Thanks to the old woman's gifts, forests and mountains rise behind the fugitives, but before they can reach the Red river, to cross which is safety, the Magician overcomes the old woman's charms. They reach the river bank only to find they cannot cross, and Fionn's magic is exhausted. But Grainnhe has a jewel, a charm against death; as long as she wears it in her hair no evil can harm her; alternatively it will give her one wish and vanish. She takes it from her hair to wish for a boat and immediately sees, as in a vision, the fate to which she will condemn herself if she gives up her talisman. But Fionn is in peril through his efforts to save her, and already she loves him, so she lays the jewel on the water. A boat at once appears and takes them to safety.

Fionn and Grainnhe are married and lived in great happiness until Grainnhe's son is about to be born. Then come messengers to Fionn to tell him that sea-pirates are attacking his small dark-skinned allies, the Sons of Morna, who have sent to remind him of his pledge to assist them. Fionn longs to remain with Grainnhe but will not break his vow. He and his men spend three days defeating the sea-pirates and when he returns Grainnhe and her baby are gone, carried off by the Grey Magician. Fionn learns from his 'tooth' that she has been turned into a hind. He searches for her for many years, but she has been sent to run with the deer in lone Glen Affaric and he never finds her. Twelve years later, when the Fiennes are hunting, their hounds pick up a scent and follow it to a small copse; Bran, who is leading, is the first to enter it, whereupon, to the surprise of all, he turns at bay, teeth bared against the Fiennes and his fellow hounds of the pack and will allow no one but Fionn to pass him. Fionn finds him guarding a wild boy, with long hair and wild, beautiful, frightened eyes, who can make only such sounds as deer make. Fionn adopts him and teaches him human speech. Needless to say, he is Grainnhe's son, but Grainnhe, the beautiful white hind of whom her son talks, is never found. After her death the Grey Magician permits her son to take her body, once more that of a woman, for burial, and the Fiennes make her grave on the summit of Beinn na Caillich, where once she ran as a hind.

It is recounted of this boy that he had in the centre of his forehead a tuft of deer's fur where his mother's tongue had licked him, and that it was from her that he got his gift of poetry. Once he was shipwrecked on Fladda and a party of hunters on the island offered him a share of their venison stew, to whom he made indignant reply: 'When everyone picks his mother's shank-bone, I will pick my mother's slender shank-bone.' The boy was Ossian.

18

Sleat

————◆■◆————

All night the witch sang, and the castle grew
Up from the rock, with tower and turret crown'd;
All night she sang—when fell the morning dew
'Twas finished round and round.

(From 'Dunskaith' by Alexander Smith)

Brindled Sleat of the beautiful women'

SLEAT, the southernmost wing of Skye, is, more than any
other wing, a distinct and separate entity, for in climate,
vegetation, and (some say) even in race, the 'Garden of
Skye' is unlike the north. Even today there is very little
intercourse between the northern and the southern ends of
the island. Probably one could find in Duirinish a hundred
men who know Glasgow and fifty who know London or
Bombay for every one who has visited Sleat, and the same
is true, of course, in Sleat regarding Duirinish. South and
north do not mix.

It has been suggested that this is a legacy from the bitter
clan wars between Macdonalds in the south and Macleods
in the north; others claim it to be due to a difference in
blood. These last claim that Sleat is inhabited to this day
by the descendants of the original small, dark-eyed inhabitants of Skye, Picts or Iberians or what you will, who
elsewhere in the island were driven underground by the
larger, though perhaps less clever, Celtic invaders and so
became the 'Little People', or fairies, who lived by magic
—or by their wits. It is certainly curious that there seem to

be no 'fairy' stories in Sleat, nor any sithein (fairy-dwellings). On the contrary, it was the Fiennes and Cuchullin in whom Sleat and Kylerhea believed, the giant people who dwelt *on* the hills (not *in* them) and were very mighty in battle. It may be, however, that the difference is chiefly geographical or, like many bigger problems, a matter of transport.

The history of Sleat is the history of the Macdonalds. It is true that in legend Cuchullin and his heroes were the first to build that fortress of many spellings now generally written Dunscaith, and certainly there was a time when all Skye, including Sleat, was Macleod country, but the Macdonalds acquired the peninsula very early in Skye history and still hold it today. If those are right who claim for Somerled that he was a Celt, at least on his mother's side, and that he and his descendants were the leaders of the Celts against the Norse invaders, it may well account for the notable difference between Sleat and the rest of Skye.

The road to Sleat takes off from the main Kyleakin–Broadford road near the township of Skulamus. For some miles it runs through bare, flat moorland ornamented by a number of small lochs, each containing one or more birch-covered islets, the haunts of wild fowl and flowers. The first point of interest is the head of Loch Eisort, which can be seen to the right. Near here the road to Drumfearn takes off. Then comes Kinloch, one of Lord Macdonald's deer forests, the Lodge (which is now an hotel) standing not far from Loch na Dal on the Sound of Sleat.

The road now winds along the coast and soon enters 'the fair woods of Duisdale', long famous in Skye, then passes Duisdale House, now an hotel. Duisdale belonged for several generations to a family of Mackinnons who held the township of Duisdale Beg for their services as standard-bearers to the Macdonalds of Sleat. From here on, till beyond Armadale, the country is quite unlike the rest of Skye. Trees abound, chiefly birch and alder; every house of any importance has its woods and lawns as in England, and these grounds contain fine, well-grown trees. Rhododendrons are plentiful and in the spring the blue-bells and primroses could vie with Kent—the Garden of England. The road is bounded in many places with the type of hedgerow which one associates with Devon lanes, hedges of hawthorn, wild rose, and elder with, on the deep banks at their roots, a mass of hartstongue fern, pisky flower, and primroses. It is interesting to note that almost every field has its name, as 'the Field of the Noisy Barnacle Geese', 'the Field of the Crooked-Smooth', and so forth, which is unusual in Skye but common in parts of rural England, where such names as 'Little Weary John' can still be heard.

Duisdale is close to Isle Ornsay, with its island (an island only at high tide), its lighthouse, township, harbour, and pier. Here the road turns inland again, passing through moorland and close to Loch nan Dubhrachan, Black Braes Loch. This loch once contained a monster, the Beast of the Little Horn, which spread such terror through the country-side that in 1870 an official search was made for it with all the appropriate gear. But no beast was found and so the problem—strayed walrus or forgotten water-horse?—was never satisfactorily settled. Close to this loch the road to Ord, Dunscaith, and Tarskavaig takes off on the right. This is a loop-road to the west of the peninsula and rejoins the main road at Ostaig.

The main road next reaches the township of Teangue, once famous for its 'withies' copse. As these birch twigs needed much preparation before they could be twisted into ropes, 'it is necessary to steep the withies' became in this district a synonym for 'it is time to go home'. Near Teangue, on the Sound of Sleat, are the ruins of Castle Camus, better known by its later name of Knock Castle. Standing on its headland, Knock was always held to be the key stronghold of Sleat and some say that but for the carelessness of the warden who held it for the Macleods and allowed himself to be surprised, the Macdonalds would never have set foot in Skye. The Macdonalds themselves made no such mistake and for a time after their landing it was the castle, as well as the chief stronghold, of the Lords of the Isles. When they eventually left it for Dunscaith it became one of the fortresses of the Barons of Sleat and stood siege from the Macleods at the end of the fifteenth century. On this occasion it was defended, and most bravely and successfully defended, by a woman, 'Mary of the Castle'. The story of how she came to be in charge has been lost, but most of the Macdonald women were dependable fighters, and the tradition of both her skill and her courage remain to this day, as also that under the shelter of her shield the clan had time to gather and to arm.

As late as 1617 Donald Gorm Macdonald held his lands in Skye from the Crown on condition that he should hold Castle Camus ever ready to receive the king or any representative the king might send. But it would seem that this 'duty' sat but lightly on the shoulders of his successors, for in 1690 we hear of Castle Camus being uninhabited, and it is now a ruin. Castle Camus possessed in its hey-day both a Gruagach (see Chapter 15) and a Glaistig, the latter in the form of a she-devil disguised as a beautiful woman, though others claim that it took the form of a grey goat. Knock had also a 'green maiden', Maighdean Uaine, believed to be the guardian spirit of the dun and of the castle's rightful

owners. She, it is believed, is still faithful to her trust and
can sometimes be seen at moonrise walking through the
ruins. Near Knock is one of the old Cheese Knolls, Cnoc
Caisse, where the Easter custom of rolling cheeses and eggs
down a grass slope was long observed.

After Knock the road runs along the coast through the
tiny townships of Saisdig and Ferindonald to Kilmore.
Near Saisdig the old priests' house stood, and so much land
went with it in those days that the priest could see a 'Skye
mile' (very long miles) of his own land whichever way he
looked out. This is the origin of many names round about,
such as 'Priest's Knoll' and the 'Knoll of the Consecrated
Wafers'. Below the present church of Kilmore is the Sgeir,
or Stone, of St. Columba. Here tradition has it that the saint
once landed and blessed the ground upon which the church
now stands. Before his time it was a place sacred to the
Druids but since then it has been Christian. It was at first
the site of an early Celtic church dedicated to the Virgin
Mary, but there is nothing to be seen now except the ivy-
clad ruin of the more modern church of Kilmore, dated
1681, together with the present church of Sleat and the old
graveyard. Here, as one might expect, is the burial-place
of the Macdonalds. The earlier Lords of the Isles, however,
were usually buried in Iona, as were many of the great
families of the North in olden days, for Iona was holy
ground and burial there ensured a happy Resurrection.

> *Isle of deeps, where death ne'er weepeth,*
> *Sails to thee a king who sleepeth,*
> *With Thy saints the Tryst he keepeth,*
> *Iomair O, 'illean-mhara*
> *Iomair O.*

('Iona Boat Song' by Kenneth Macleod)

The grandest funeral ever seen in Skye was that of Sir Alexander Macdonald of Sleat, upon which £2,634 was spent. He was a good chief and did much for his people, as did his wife, the beloved Lady Margaret, whose funeral was almost as large as Flora Macdonald's. Sir Alexander it was whose participation in the Rising of 1715 resulted in the forfeiture of his estates, however, and it is told of him that after the '45 (when he wished to raise the clan for King George but was advised that it was impossible) he visited the Duke of Cumberland at Inverness. The Duke greeted him with would-be wit: 'Is this the great rebel of the Isles?', to which Sir Alexander made reply: 'My Lord Duke, had I been the rebel of the Isles Your Royal Highness had never crossed the Spey.'

He was believed to have written to Macdonald of Kingsburgh telling him that the Prince would almost certainly seek shelter at Kingsburgh and that, if he did, he (Macdonald of Kingsburgh) should remember how greatly to his advantage it would be to sell him to Cumberland's men. What the letter did actually contain was never known, as Kingsburgh destroyed it, but neither writer nor recipient denied its purport and many never forgave Sir Alexander for what they held to be 'low treachery'. Few men can have died more deeply mourned and more bitterly hated. Two epitaphs composed on the occasion of his death and both said to have been recited in Kilmore graveyard are interesting:

> *A model of the human kind;*
> *A body faultless and a faultless mind.*
>
> .   .   .   .   .
>
> *Great, good and regular his every part,*
> *His form majestic, godlike was his heart.*

That was one; here is the other:

> *If Heaven be pleased when sinners cease to sin,*
> *If Hell be pleased when sinners enter in,*
> *If Earth be pleased to quit a truckling knave,*
> *Then all be pleased; Macdonald's in his grave.*

Through greenland and woodland the road passes on to Kilbeg, once the site of a tiny Celtic chapel or cell, and Ostaig. The old house of Ostaig, once famous alike for its library and its hospitality, is now a ruin, but it was here that Dr. Johnson stayed as the guest of Dr. Martin Macpherson, then minister of Sleat, a son-in-law of Mackinnon of Corry. Here the Doctor and Boswell were storm-stayed for five days, waiting to cross to the mainland, which they finally succeeded in doing on 3 October 1773. During those five days much discussion of Macpherson's 'Ossian' took place, and in what better setting than Ossian's own country? But curiously enough in that long and detailed discussion no one appears to have noticed, or anyhow to have commented upon, the extraordinary difference in the character of Cuchullin in the two cycles. In the Irish cycle, 'The Tarn of Cuchullin', Cuchullin is a 'great hero', larger than life, a young warrior joying in his strength, with no ideas beyond fighting and being feted of all men. Magic he uses. Indeed he is half of another world and half true Irish. He has only to enter a battle to be victorious, to look at a woman to make her love him. In the Ossian stories, on the other hand, Cuchullin is a man torn between love for his wife and his duty to the child King of Ulster, whose guardian he is. Duty wins and he is defeated and then killed in saving Ulster, but his heart remains in Dunscaith, his home.

It was to Mrs. Macpherson of Ostaig that a woman,

reputed to have been rather simple, is said to have composed the song 'Ho Ro, Mhairi Dhubh'. This woman may have been 'Old Marcellie', a very well-known character in her day. She was childlike and simple but quite harmless, she dressed always, winter and summer, in white, never spent more than one night under one roof. On arrival she asked for soap and water and washed everything she had on ; then and not till then would she eat, talk, and 'wait upon' the lady of the house. A welcome awaited her everywhere, for was she not the B.B.C. and the local newspaper rolled into one ? Her surname is forgotten but she was believed to be kin to almost every family in the island.

The new house of Ostaig, close to the shore near the branch road to Tarskavaig, is at present the home of Lord and Lady Macdonald, and not far beyond stands Armadale Castle, a beautiful eighteenth-century house in castle style in its lovely 'southern' setting of woods and lawns. Two things are most noticeable about these grounds ; the beauty, height, and straightness of the trees, many of them varieties seldom if ever before grown in the Hebrides ; and secondly the ferns. The woods are green with them : ferns of every sort and kind native to Britain. Both in mass of actual plants and in number of varieties it appears easily to excel the world-famous 'Fern Gulley' of Jamaica, while the trees with their boughs laden with fern parasites bear close resemblance to the orchid-laden trees of the tropics.

When Armadale was built and by whom seems a somewhat controversial question. Alexander Mackenzie in his *History of the Macdonalds* says it was built by Sir Alexander Wentworth of Sleat, who was born in 1775. But in *An Account of the Highland Clans*, published in 1725 (exactly fifty years earlier), we find that though Duntulm was given as the chief residence, 'Armodel' was mentioned also, the words being: 'They have also another place of residence, adorned with stately edifices, pleasant gardens and other regular policies called Armodel.' Yet earlier still (in 1690) we hear that Armadale House was burned by the King's fleet. Obviously, if it could be burned it must previously have been built. Probably there were two Armadales, first a house and later the castle with its Strath marble and English stained glass. Possibly 'Port an Tigh Mhoir' (the Port of the Great House) a little farther up the coast commemorates the site of the earlier building.

The tale of the burning is as follows. In 1690 the forfeiture of the Macdonald estates was ordered by King William because the Macdonald of the day had not only fought for James but, after William and Mary were proclaimed sovereigns, still refused to swear fealty or even to keep the peace. King William is said to have made many approaches with a view to winning Sir Donald Macdonald's allegiance, or at least ending active disturbances, but without success. Finally two frigates were sent to Skye with orders not to use force if it could be avoided but, if necessary, to serve upon him 'the forfeiture of his estates'. They tried conciliation. They tried to persuade him to parley. But Sir Donald would not receive them or their messages. At last the order was given to the crews to land at Creag a Chaim, near Armadale, and burn Armadale House. When the flames were seen, Sleat rose as one man and marched upon the fire-raisers, who fled to Castle Camus, then standing empty, there to defend themselves, but through lack of supplies they had at length to surrender and were all hanged. Another party reached the Mound of Dun Flo near Tormore and there defended themselves fiercely, led by a Royalist officer who was so powerful a swordsman that he held off all comers until finally killed by an axe tied to a fishing-rod and wielded from a rock behind the Mound. This party, too, was exterminated. And yet, in spite of all this, Macdonald's forfeiture lasted only for a very short period and in 1691 we hear of Sir Donald swearing fealty to the reigning monarch.

Dr. Johnson's first visit in Skye was to Armadale (but not, I think, to Armadale House), where he was the guest of Sir Alexander and Lady Macdonald, who had postponed a visit to the south in order to receive him. Dr. Johnson has since been much criticized for his comments on his host on this occasion.

Beyond Armadale is Ardvasar, a large township on Armadale Bay. Near here is Dun na Ceard, the Craftsmen's Dun. This seems to be the nearest approach to a sithein (fairy hill) in Sleat. In it or on it lived the wondrous craftsmen who could convert any piece of iron or of wood, brought to them at night, to any other purpose. To test them a man once brought a lint mallet to be made into a spear-shaft. All night long they were heard lamenting while they hammered: 'My distress and calamity, oh my distress and calamity; make a spear-shaft out of a beetle (lint mallet).'

Not far from Ardvasar is tiny Port na Faganaich, the Port (or Bay) of the Forsaken Ones. Here some great stones stand in the sea. One story tells how they were thrown there by the Fiennes when they were exercising in Knoydart: another makes them pagans who, having 'hearts of stone', would not repent at St. Columba's preaching, nor be baptized, and so became in time 'all stone like their hearts'. But the third story goes better with the Gaelic name. It tells how one night a party of young fishermen returning late from their fishing saw something splashing in the phosphorescent water. They approached quietly and found a number of seal-maidens who had sloughed off their seal-skins and were disporting themselves in the sea. So lovely were they that the youths stood entranced, all but one who ran away with their skins. As the first shafts of dawn light pierced the sky the maidens made for the rock, only to find themselves skinless. They wept and lamented and the boys, in honest ignorance of the skins' whereabouts, comforted them as best they could. To cut a long story short, each seal-maiden married a young fisherman and they lived together in much happiness for a year, then the youth who had hidden the seal-skins had it 'laid upon him' to return them. That night came the call of the sea and the seal-maidens obeyed it. They could do no other. Their husbands, trying to hold them back, were turned into stones when they entered the sea with their wives. But the seal-maidens never forget and can be seen, by those who have the eyes to see, in the soft sea moonlight, each keeping tryst with her own stone.

About a mile beyond these stones stands Tormore House. On the shore close to it is the Mound of Dun Flo, or Dun Chlo, site of the massacre already mentioned. At Tormore the good road ends but a third-class one goes on along the coast, through the township of Calligarry and past the site of Dun a Chleirich, to the Aird of Sleat with its township. Here the road ends at Port na Long, shortly before the Point of Sleat. Port na Long was once the main port of Sleat and a harbour of some importance in Skye. On the Point of Sleat itself is supposed to have been a volcano, the last active one in the West, according to tradition. It is said to have blown itself and much land into the sea, thereby separating the Isle of Eigg from Sleat. Until fairly modern times the people of the Aird were a people apart, very tall and fair. They were nicknamed 'Na Faoileagan', the Seagulls, as being supposed to live chiefly on this bird.

There is no road up the western side of the peninsula from Point of Sleat to Tarskavaig, though it is beautiful country with wonderful views. Beyond the road end is the site of another little Celtic church, then comes Carradale (Copse-wood-dale). This wood was long believed to be inhabited by an enormous bird, such as was never seen in Skye before or since.

> *There's a great bird in Carradale*
> *With a home it has in Earnasgal;*
> *Its neighbour's house so far away*
> *It cannot go and call on him.*

Not far from here is a big hill pond or tiny loch, Lochan na Poite; in it is sunk a brass creel filled with gold which shall only be recovered when the 'three things which are to be have been'. It was once guarded by a monster but he was killed and buried in Lagan Inis na Cnaimh, the Hollow of the Meadow of Bones; here, four or five generations ago, the bones of some prehistoric or other large extinct creature were in fact found.

Still farther up the west coast lies Tarskavaig township, a name said to mean Whale Bay. Here the road from Ostaig, which passes Loch Dhugaill and the valley of the Gillean Burn (a road of beautiful views) comes in. Close to Tarskavaig, guarding the little bay of 'Ob Gauscavaig, stand the ruins of Dunscaith, said to mean the Fort of Gloom. It is believed that the castle was, in fact, a great deal larger then the fragments that remain would indicate, but even these serve to show what an impregnable fortress it must once have been. For several centuries it was the castle and stronghold of the Macdonalds of the Isles, but in lenged it was much older than any clan, as it probably was in fact also. Most Skye duns have their origin in Neolithic or even earlier times.

In Macpherson's 'Ossian' it is at Dunscaith that Cuchullin lands when he first comes to Skye, and Skye, not Ireland, is the home and love of his manhood. In the Ossian story Cuchullin and his heroes build Dunscaith in a single night to be his dwelling. He becomes, among other titles, 'Car-borne Chief of Dunscai' and 'Chief of the Isle of Mist'. It is here, to Dunscaith, that he brings his bride Bragela, daughter of 'Car-borne Sorglan', and here he lives with her in great happiness. Then comes word that an enemy, the King of Lochlin (Scandinavia), is on his way to attack Ulster, whose king is the child Cormac, Cuchullin's ward. Cuchullin must go to its defence. The other Ulster chiefs are scattered, hunting, raiding, and so forth, and Cuchullin and his men are far outnumbered. They fight bravely from dawn to dusk but win no decisive victory. That night Cuchuilin bids the bards sing to him of Bragela.

> *Oh strike the harp in praise of my love,*
> *The lonely sunbeam of Dunscaith.*
> *Strike the harp in praise of Bragela,*
> *She I left in the Isle of Mist.*
> *Dost thou raise thy fair face from the rock*
> *To find the sails of Cuchullin?*
>
>   ·   ·   ·   ·
>
> *Retire, for it is night, my love;*
> *The dark wind sings in thy hair,*
> *Retire to the halls of my feasts*
> *Think of the times that are past.*
> *I will not return till the storm of war is ceased.*

Next day a second great battle is fought. Fingal, who

with his men, is on his way from Scotland to help Cuchullin, is held up by contrary winds. The chiefs of Ulster are not yet returned. Once more Cuchullin and his heroes fight alone, but this time they meet with defeat as the sun goes down and Cuchullin laments that night in his tent:

> *And thou, white bosomed Bragela,*
> *Mourn over the fall of my fame:*
> *Vanquished I will never return to thee*
> *Thou sunbeam of my soul.*

On the third day they fight once more. Cuchullin and his men are exhausted and can no longer hold the Northmen. Cuchullin sees many of his friends and heroes killed. Then Fingal arrives. Though defeated, Cuchullin has gained time and saved Ulster, but he is sad for his friends who have fallen, and for his own defeat. He sends his sword to Fingal, as one no longer fit to wear it, and laments:

Oh Bragela thou art too far remote
To cheer the heart of a hero;
But let him see thy bright form in his mind
That his thoughts may return to the lonely sunbeam of his love.

Fingal returns Cuchullin's sword and tries to convince him that he, and he alone, has saved Ulster. But, seeing him utterly cast down and exhausted, he then tries to persuade him to return to Skye and leave the next day's battle to him and his Fiennes.

> *Spread now thy white sails for the Isle of Mist*
> *See Bragela leaning on her rock*
> *Her tender eye is in tears*
>
> .   .   .   .   .
>
> *She listens to the breeze of night*
> *To hear the voice of thy rowers.*

But Cuchullin, foreseeing his own death, replies:

> *Long shall she listen in vain*
> *Cuchullin shall never return.*

Bragela sits watching and mourning:

> *Is it the white wave on the rock*
> *And not Cuchullin's sails?*
> *Often do the mists deceive me for the ship of my love.*

Cuchullin is killed in battle and Bragela dies of a broken heart in the 'Hall of Shells'. And as Dunscaith was built in a single night, so it falls back into ruin.

Other tales make Cuchullin fall in love with Scia's daughter Aoife and some say that Bragela (Fair bosom) was Cuchullin's name for her. She bore him a son, Conlach. Others again claim that as he landed he saw Uathach, daughter of the Princess of the Dun, look forth from her window. He loved and married her and inherited the Dun.

Near Dunscaith is still shown the great stone to which Cuchullin used to tie his dog Luath after hunting.

A different tradition about Dunscaith makes it a fort built by the Fienne giants and later occupied for a short time by a Roman ship's company. But history shows it to have been a vitrified fort of early importance and, later, the chief stronghold in the south, first of the Macleods and then of the Macdonalds of Sleat. There is a belief that the present ruined keep was superimposed upon the old vitrified fort in about 1266. In the time of the Macleods, the Mac-Askells were 'Wardens of Dunscaith', and so well are they reputed to have discharged this and other duties laid upon them that they received from the chief of Clan Macleod a somewhat unusual reward (see Chapter 7). Later, when

Sleat fell into Macdonald hands, the chiefs soon left Castle Camus for Dunscaith and it continued as their main castle and fortress until after the Battle of Trotternish, when they moved to Duntulm, the more easily to protect their recent gains. The stories which have come down to us of those centuries of Macdonald occupation are wild indeed.

One of the earlier stories told concerns a Macdonald chief who, after one of the many Macdonald-Macleod wars, made peace with his neighbours and gave a daughter in marriage to one of Macleod's sons. The girl had other views and opposed the marriage furiously, but was not consulted. In due course she had two sons, but her hatred of her husband and her father remained unabated. One day the whole family returned to Dunscaith for a visit, Macdonald being, it was believed, very devoted to the two boys, his only grandchildren. He and young Macleod went out hunting. On their return they were met, to their surprise, by a smiling wife, who told them to hurry as she had herself prepared such a savoury fawn pasty as they had never tasted. Hungry, they ate well and praised her handiwork. Then she sprang up and crying, '*Now* you know my devotion. I have cooked my children for your dinner and you have eaten them. No heirs for Macdonald. No heirs for Macleod', she flung herself from the window on to the rocks below.

In 1449, when certain lands in Skye were formally acknowledged to be Macdonald property, Hugh of Sleat dwelt at Dunscaith and from then onwards the castle had a history of battles round its walls and of sieges and forays. But there was little of special note until Dunscaith passed to a collateral descendant of Hugh's, Donald Gruamach (the Grim) who married a Clanranald and lived at Dunscaith.

Once, while she was entertaining twelve of her kinsmen, a cousin of Donald Gruamach's, Ranald Macdonald from North Uist, arrived to visit them. He stayed the night but very early the following morning prepared to depart. Donald protested at the shortness of his visit and the early hour of his departure and finally remarked: 'Stay at least to say farewell to my wife.' 'If I stay she will not thank me', replied Ranald, and hurried off. In due course the hostess arose and went to her window; there, displayed for her regard, were hung the twelve corpses of her kinsmen, slain by Ranald, who (it is thought) must have had a feud with the family. Lady Macdonald did *not* thank him; on the contrary, she sent her steward to assassinate him, which task he duly accomplished. The Macdonalds left Dunscaith for Duntulm about 1539.

The road from Tarskavaig to Ord is very wild and very beautiful. It consists of a series of steep and twisty hills; on the right, moorland and little lochs, trees and wild, turbulent peat burns, and, on the left, views of Dunscaith on its crag, with the Cuchullins and Blaaven across the water of Loch Eisort as a background. Later, it runs through a natural wood of oak, hazel, and birch, now marked on the map as Wood of Tokavaig but once a sacred grove whose old name of Doir'an Druidean is still remembered, though the ancient trees have perished. Doir'an Druidean (or Tradain) has been translated as the Grove of Quarrelling, or of Starlings, or of Druids. A later name was Doire Ghoan, probably Grove of Choan (St. Comgan). Tradition has no doubts of the meaning, however: it was a sacred grove of the Druids and here an ancient deity was worshipped. Into this grove the Beast from Loch an Doirenach (said to mean Loch of the Grove of the Horse) used to walk in the form of a horse, and here

it was always killed with a silver knife, but whether it was
a water-horse or a Druid sacrifice is not clear. Anyhow, St.
Comgan, when he visited Sleat, blessed the grove, and the
horse was never again seen.

Not far from here is Cnoc na Fuarachad, the Hill of Cold,
and near it the River of Cold (or Death), across which the
dead were carried, though why is again not clear. Perhaps
it was another name for the Ord river and the hill upon
which stand the ruins of the little church of St. Chaon with
its ancient graveyard, or perhaps it had some connexion
with that other small river which runs out to sea between
the two burial-mounds of Inveraulavaig. Here the 'Great
Ones of the Dun' are buried. Whether 'the Dun' was Dunscaith or the sacred grove no one now remembers, but
the name of Olaf is associated with this burn.

The road finally crosses the Ord river where the big pearl
mussels (called dog mussels) used to abound. On the north
bank lie the ruins of tiny Teampuill Chaon which face, as
exactly as may be, the Teampuill Chaon of Boreraig on the
opposite shore of Loch Eisort, likewise now a ruin. Close to
the little chapel were once the two springs Tobar an
Domhnaich (Well of the Lord) and Tobar na Sliante (Well
of Health); near them stood the 'Stone of Healing' also. It
would seem that though small, this chapel must once have
been of some importance. Its holy-water stoup was for long
preserved in Ord House. Tradition claims that the sanctity
of this spot goes back to long before the Christian era. St.
Comgan, it is said, came to Sleat specially to bless and
consecrate the Well and Stone of Healing, but their healing
gifts were far older than the saint. In those far-away days
they were surrounded by a sacred wood and were treated
with the respect they deserved. But times change, and the
day came when an unbeliever visited the Well of Healing

and washed his dirty hands in the good water to show himself superior alike to healing waters and ordinary courtesy. St. Choan saw and was displeased, and as the man rose to his feet, shaking his hands to dry them, the drops fell on dry ground. The healing spring had vanished, but not for ever. It soon gushed forth again, crystal clear and pure, no longer on the chapel hill but below it on the sea-shore. Here it can still be seen, though its water is now piped to the Ord Hotel annexe. The Well of the Lord has also disappeared, but a curious circle of stone near the site of the old church may be the place where the water once rose.

Ord itself is Fienne country. A tiny bay near by commemorates in its name, Bay of the Dwarf, the 'grey lad' or 'lad of skins' who stole the Cup of Worth for Fionn and who now haunts this, his landing-place. On the nearby rocky islet, Sgeir Ghormoil, now a seal nursery, the blue-eyed Fienne maiden Gormshuil was imprisoned by the evil giant Mocaidh, who dwelt on the Ridge of Ord and was bright yellow. In the sea near it is the great boulder he 'cast out by a slight knock of his ankle' to swamp her lover when he tried to rescue her. Near here, too, roamed the wild boar which Diarmid killed in Gleann na Beiste, and at Ord is Creag a Bheoir, Crag of Beer. On it beer was made from birch juice by a recipe traditionally handed down from the days of the giants and which remained in use there until whisky eclipsed it.

Ord itself stands on a steep rise on the north bank of the river; from it on a clear day can be seen one of Skye's lovelier views. The house, like so many others in Skye, is now an hotel. In the days of the Napoleonic Wars it is said that one house in Skye contributed more men to the war than any other house in Britain. Be that as it may, the

Loch Slapin from Ord, Blaaven in cloud

Kilchriosd

island certainly sent over 10,000 men, 600 captains, and many officers of higher rank, and the survivors were widespread over Skye. One of these was Charles Macdonald of Ord, the 'Old Ord' of Alexander Smith's *A Summer in Skye*. His grandfather, Macdonald of Gillan, a man of immense strength, had been 'out' in the '45 and distinguished himself by breaking in the great gates of Carlisle, so he became an outlaw with a price on his head and his lands were forfeited. He was married 'in the hills' and his son was born there, an outlaw like his father, and christened by a priest who risked his life to do it, yet the grandson served the Crown in every war he could find, from the West Indies via Ireland to Waterloo. His title to fame in Skye, however, is chiefly the Ord Palm. A man named Murdo, who had worked for him for many years, emigrated to New Zealand with his family in 1863. On arrival there he collected a number of seeds of a palm which he particularly admired, called, I am told, the Cabbage Tree (it is not the Cabbage Palm of South America) and sent them to 'Old Ord'. Some of these seeds were planted in the old walled garden at Ord and some were sent to the Botanical Gardens at Kew. Those sent to Kew died from frost but two of those planted at Ord had luck in three mild winters while young and they flourished and are still to be seen, being, as far as is known, the only specimens ever grown in the open in Britain. They are now, at eighty years old, well-grown trees about fifteen to twenty feet high. Every seventh year they flower and become a mass of deep creamy blossom, so heavily scented that not only the whole garden but the house some little distance away appears temporarily transported to the tropics. A relative of Murdo met some of his descendants in New Zealand recently and they immediately inquired for the Cabbage Tree.

Flax was a great crop at Ord, too, in the old days, and the household linen was spun at home a hundred years ago, but the smell of the rotting flax was a very different scent and was so unpopular with his wife and family that after Old Ord's death its cultivation was given up.

Ord is said to have possessed the first fixed bath (with hot and cold water) in Skye; the old bath, made of lead and with right-angle corners like a box, which remained in use until 1950, was well worth a visit. But apart from Ord House that corner of Skye seems to have been very backward in Old Ord's day. 'Black' kitchens were still usual, and his eldest son, who had a great dislike of women with thick ankles, used, if he met any while riding in the district, to order them off the road. And they would go. This within living memory.

Sleat was reputed to be the original home of the belief that Gaelic was the universal language before the Tower of Babel was begun.

> When Adam first his Eve did meet,
> Shimmering bright as morning dew,
> The first words he spoke to her
> Were 'Ciamar tha thu'n daugh'
> ('How are you today?')

After Ord the road runs inland through birch woods to the main Armadale road once more, passing on its right the Kelpie's Loch, so called because of the adventure of a young couple who were once returning to Tarskavaig from a marriage at Ardvasar. As they were passing close to this little loch, what was their horror to see a stirring of the surface and then the head of a water-horse rising among the lilies. The young man took to his heels and his wife did her best to follow him, but, hampered by the long skirts of the period, she was soon overtaken by the kelpie, half man, half horse. The girl was utterly terrified and cried out to her husband to save her, but he continued his headlong flight. 'Don't be frightened', begged the water-horse kindly, as he carried her off, 'better half a man than one who is no man at all.'

19

Strath

Still and untroubled sits the Kingly One
Yonder the eagle floats—there sleeps the snow
Against the pale green of the cloudless sky.

(From 'King Blaabheinn' (Blaaven) by
Robert Buchanan)

THE district of Strath always seems to stand alone. For instance, it is not unusual to talk of North Skye and South Skye, but South Skye in common speech has come to mean Sleat, and Strath is most certainly not North Skye. Equally, it is left out when the expressions 'Macleod land' and 'Macdonald land' are used. Strath was neither. Broadford and the valley of Strath behind it, Strathaird and Corry, were all 'Mackinnon country'. How the Mackinnons survived in Strath is something of a mystery. The story of Skye is the story of endless clan wars and battles between the two great clans of Macdonald and Macleod which divided the island between them. Probably it would be hard to find a square mile on which no members of these clans had ever fought. And between them lay the tiny sept of Mackinnons of Corry and Strath—or rather, sometimes between them and sometimes surrounded as frontiers were pushed forward or driven back, yet never, it seems, becoming a Naboth's vineyard to either neighbour, attractive as that bay and fertile valley must have been.

Most clans had some nickname, usually uncomplimentary, bestowed upon them by others: 'Murdering Mac-

donalds', 'Treacherous Campbells', 'Stab in-the-back Mac-
cleans), and such. The Mackinnons of Skye were known as
the 'Two-faced', and no doubt they had need to be! Clever,
tactful, and brave they must have been to remain in possession of their own land through the centuries. They married
Macleods and they married Macdonalds, they spoke both
fair and were of service to both and yet remained always
independent.

It is strange how little the Mackinnons of Strath and
Broadford have been noticed in story, however. For instance, everyone who has heard of the '45 has heard of
Flora Macdonald and of the Prince's pilot, Donald Macleod
of Galtrigal, but few have heard of the Mackinnons' share
in the matter. Yet it was Mackinnon who hid the Prince
when the hunt was closing in and even his last guide, Malcolm Macleod of Raasay, had been taken prisoner.

Strath appears to have been a great religious centre ever
since prehistoric times. The remains of several stone circles
are still to be seen there, in close juxtaposition to a number
of ancient churches now in ruins. It seems generally agreed
that before St. Columba brought Christianity to Skye the
pagan religion of the island was that mysterious cult which
has come to us only in the form of stone circles (believed to
have been places of worship), monoliths (which in Skye
seem to have been frequently connected with graves or
burial-grounds), and sacred wells and woods, the latter
usually hazel groves. St. Columba never attempted to
destroy the sacred places of paganism nor the firm belief in
the virtues of certain harmless practices he found: instead
he blessed them and gave them a Christian symbolism, as
in the story of St. Turog and the wells at Flodigarry (see
Chapter 5). This is very clearly illustrated in Strath,
where five old churches or chapels, now ruins, stand each

beside or near a stone circle, and the graveyards all contain some prehistoric stones as well as having the tradition that they were first pagan burial-grounds and later Christian.

The road to Elgol takes off from the main road at Broadford Hotel and follows the valley of the Broadford river as far as Loch Chriosd, looking up at one of the beauties of Strath, the Red Hills Beinn na Caillich and Beinn Dearg. About a mile from Broadford the first place of interest can be seen, the ruins of the old house of Corriecatachan (Corrie of the Cats) which lies beyond the river. Here we are indeed in Mackinnon country and here it was that the Mackinnons of Corry entertained Dr. Johnson and Boswell when they visited Skye in 1773. Boswell's account of the visit is too well known to require repetition, but family tradition has handed down one story not usually recorded. Dr. Johnson appeared to be enjoying his dinner, which consisted of a local Skye dish of the period which closely resembled Irish stew but was made with partially salted mutton. His hostess remarked: 'I hope you like this dish, Sir?' to which the Doctor made polite reply: 'Madam, this food is only fit for hogs.' 'Then won't you have some more?' was the instant retort, which caused Dr. Johnson to tell Anable Mackinnon that her mother was the wittiest woman he had ever met. The Doctor's astonishment at finding that the older members of the party at Corriecatachan spoke Latin together when they did not wish to be understood by the children or the maids, as well as Gaelic to the said maids, is still remembered.

Corriecatachan was the only house in Skye which Dr. Johnson visited twice and it is interesting to note how much impressed he was by the number of books he found there, for the fame of another Skye library of that time

lives to this day, the library of Mackinnon's son-in-law the
Rev. Dr. Macpherson, at Ostaig.

Perhaps the best view of Corriecatachan is to be had from
the top of Aant Sithe, a green mound close to the roadway
on the right-hand side. This, as its name implies, is a fairy
place. On clear moonlight nights the fairies can be seen
dancing on the grass that surrounds the central stone and
anyone approaching quietly and with a receptive mind
may hear the wonderful strains of fairy music issuing from
the ground. What the mound was before it was a fairy
dwelling is something of a mystery. In the centre of the
summit stands a large stone, perhaps once a 'standing-
stone' but now closely resembling a broken tooth. Round
it is a ring of grass, and then a ring of stone much over-
grown; from this stone ring or circle run causeways (or
perhaps old fortifications or walls), like the rays of a star,
to the low ground around it.

Not far from Aant Sithe the road passes the old churchyard and ruined church of Kilchriosd. Standing on a small
mound by the roadside, the ruins of Kilchriosd Church are
most picturesque, partially ivy-clad and partially covered
(most unusual in Skye, this) with a thick coat of cotone-
asters, whose dark leaves and crimson berries give a curious
and unusual warmth to the scene.

There is an amusing tale told of the old churchyard at
Kilchriosd. Some boys desired to frighten an old soldier of
the Peninsular War whose way home at dusk took him
close to the burial-ground, so one night the youths, draping
themselves in sheets, hid among the tombstones and sprang
out to meet him with ghostly groans. The old man, however, was more than a match for them and exclaiming:
'You have not been long buried; you are too fresh whatever!', he lifted his stick and laid about him manfully. At

the same time he called upon the ghosts of his ancestors to rise from their graves in the churchyard and come to his help. The boys, greatly fearing his prayer might be answered, fled for dear life and, it was said, dared not again approach the spot even in broad daylight. The old man went home chuckling.

This ancient graveyard is certainly older than the church itself and possibly older even than the stone circle near by. Most Skye burial-grounds are very old, partly perhaps because people have died since time immemorial and the number of suitable sites for a graveyard in Skye are strictly limited, but perhaps also because St. Columba never broke old customs and we, as a people, are very conservative. It is said that this burial-ground once contained an enormous cross, fifty-four feet long, but, if so, there is no trace of it now. Several interesting grave-slabs with the usual Celtic designs engraved on them can still be seen, however, and at one end of the ruined church is an enclosure containing the family burial-place of the Mackinnons of Corry.

About half a mile beyond the ruins of Kilchriosd lies Loch Cil Chriosd. This loch seems to have been held in more than ordinary veneration from the earliest times. Near it, and not far from the road, a stone circle can still be seen, by no means so well preserved as those in the Lews but undoubtedly a circle, and traditionally a prehistoric 'temple'. Close to this circle is the site of the very early and tiny church of Kilcro, Church (or Cell) of the Circle, supposed to have been built on a site chosen by St. Columba himself and first occupied by the cell of one of his followers. Near it is an ancient graveyard and here two very old and curious stones were once to be seen; one was said to bear a striking resemblance to a heathen or pagan idol or Cromcreaich.

Once, Loch Cil Chriosd was haunted by a terrible monster (perhaps the pagan god Lugh himself?), which laid waste the land round about and carried off and devoured women and children. At last the creature was laid by St. Maelrhuba blessing the waters, ever since when the water of that loch has had certain virtues and healing powers. But some have believed that Loch Cil Chriosd was (or sprang from) that cursed stream 'beyond Drum Albyn in the country of the Picts' mentioned in Adamnan's *Life of St. Columba*. This spring, 'which senseless men, the Druids blinding their understanding, worshipped as a god', was believed to have the power to cause leprosy, blindness, or intense weakness in those who washed in its water or drank it. The evil spirit in the water was propitiated by many sacrifices until St. Columba came to the loch side and, knowing its evil reputation, blessed the water and then both drank from it and washed. Adamnan states that a company of Druids stood by overjoyed, eagerly waiting for the god to show his powers. But the saint took no harm, and since his blessing the waters have been pure and good for all men.

To the left of the road lies Glen Suardal. In the olden days, before Clan Mackinnon came to Skye, this is said to have been the chief abode of the family of Gillies, who then held most of what is now Strath and much of Bracadale. Indeed, some have associated them with St. Maelrhuba, since their territorial interests and boundaries appear somewhat similar. Later, a farm in Suardal was allotted by Mackinnon of Strathaird to the MacInneses, who were his hereditary archers. It is still known, in Gaelic, as 'Archer's Meadow'. Overshadowing Suardal and the head of Loch Slapin lies Beinn an Dubhaich, a mountain famous for its marble, white, grey, and black. At one time this was much sought after, being said to be of even finer texture than the

Italian. Strath marble was used for the chief altar in Iona
and, if tradition is to be believed, also in the building of the
Vatican and of the Palace of Versailles. It was used, too, in
many of the older Skye houses, including Armadale Castle.
The old Manse of Strath is said to have been built entirely
of the white and grey.

Soon after Loch Cil Chriosd the road begins to rise and
passes a small lochan. Near here is the site of the old church
of Kilbride, the ruins of which have now almost entirely
disappeared, though a little way beyond it traces of a stone
circle, certainly very much earlier, can still be seen. The
site of Kilbride is not visible from the road, but near it, on
the glebe of the new parish church of Torran, stands the
Annat Stone. This is an immense boulder of upright shape
and of it the Brahn Seer prophesied: 'Here the raven will
drink his fill of blood from the Stone.' The Stone is reputed
to have once been thirty feet high but now it is but five or
six—anyhow, above ground. Like the Temple of Annait in
Waternish, this Annat Stone is a mystery. Near it is Tobar
an h'annait, the Well of Annat.

The site of the little church of Kilbride must have been
well suited to its saint, for was it not she who miraculously
foretold St. Columba's birth and how he should become 'a
great tree whose top should reach over Erin and Albania
[Scotland]'? And her bird, the oyster-catcher, 'Servant of
Bride', still circles overhead. Near here lay Tigh-nan-
Druinich, House of the Craftsmen. The place so named was
a small, round, stone house, built chiefly underground,
though the little aperture which served as its door was, of
course, on the surface but well hidden. These tiny dwellings
were once common in Skye and known as Picts' houses.
They are reputed to have been occupied by a race of very
small men; indeed, the little entrance-holes, being assumed

by some to be ordinary doorways, gave rise to tales of a
people eighteen to twenty inches high. These people were
believed to live lives of contemplation, each by himself in
his small hidden house, and to emerge only after dark. Nevertheless, they were held to be highly skilled craftsmen who
had a school called Druinechus, where they were employed
by both St. Patrick and St. Columba as embroiderers of
vestments. They have sometimes been confused with
Druids, a very different people. Another name for Tigh-
nan-Druinich was Fideacha-de-De, Green Isle of God.

After Kilbride the road runs through the township of
Torran, twisting down the mountainside until it reaches
the shore of Loch Slapin near the loch's head. As it twists
and turns, one of the most beautiful views in Skye opens
out: far below lies Loch Slapin, blue and silver in the sunshine, indigo and purple where the mountains lie mirrored.
Beyond can be seen the open sea, with the Islands of Eigg
and Rhum guarding the entrance; farther away still lies
Soay, famous alike for its stone and its sharks. To the north
brood the Cuchullins.

The road crosses Strath Bheag, passing near Clach Oscar,
though this cannot be seen from the roadway. This great
stone commemorates one of the Fienne giants, Oscar, that
illustrious one 'whose banner never went a foot back until
the grey earth trembled'. He is reputed to have flung the
stone there from a neighbouring hilltop when suffering
from high spirits.

Next the road passes round the head of the loch and across
the foot of the 'great glen', Strath Mhor; here at specially
high tide the sea covers the roadway for two or three miles,
as is testified by the masses of seaweed on the moorland
beyond it. The Strath Mhor is really a land continuation of
Loch Slapin and in it are a chain of small lochs. The largest

of these, Loch Sguabaidh, was inhabited for years by a famous water-horse whose chief occupation was carrying off any pretty girl who ventured within his reach. Plain girls were thought to be safe from him: indeed, so good was his taste held to be that any girl who was pursued by him and escaped had her reputation as a beauty assured. Some believe that this water-horse was the 'beast' killed by Mackinnon of Strath in Bealach na Beiste, the Pass of the Beast, as it made its way by this pass between Garbh Bheinn and Belig to the shores of Lochna Creitheach, intent on mischief.

Of all the mountains and hills of Skye, and perhaps of Scotland, Blaaven has been the most often described and is the hero of the most poems. Those who have only seen Blaaven as one of the great range of the Cuchullins, red and black, may be surprised, but anyone who has taken the Elgol road will understand. For the road runs on close under the feet of Blaaven, beautiful at all times, wonderful beyond words in his winter snow coat, condescending out of the great silence to the little men in their little cars who are breaking his peace.

Soon the road crosses the Dunach burn (Burn of Misfortune) which is said to have got its somewhat inauspicious name as follows. Once upon a time seven girls and a young boy went to spend the summer in a shieling up above the waterfall where the burn rises. The girls went out to a wedding, leaving the child alone. In came seven large cats, seated themselves by the fire, and talked. The boy watched, amazed. Then the cats arose, took all the good from the butter and the cream, leaving but the appearance, and vanished. When the girls came home the frightened boy told his story and they, seeing, as they thought, butter and cream in plenty, laughed at his dream. Next night, back came the cats, and by the dawning all the girls were dead. Later that day their mothers came, as was the custom, to fetch the butter and cream. And each in turn, as she entered and saw the dead girls, cried out: 'Airidh mo dunach' (the Shieling of Misfortune).

Having crossed the Dunach burn the road runs for two or three miles across Druim an Fhuarain, so called from Clachan Fhuarain (the Well Stone), an enormous stone, estimated to weigh over two tons, which one of Cuchullin's companions flung here when he was practising 'putting the weight' in the Isle of Soay. This again is not to be seen from the roadway, but many and glorious views are.

Some miles beyond the Dunach burn the road leaves the loch side and turns inland towards Strathaird House. Between it and the sea lies Dun Ringill. Dun Ringill Castle was originally the Mackinnon stronghold and is reputed to have been occupied as early as the ninth century. It was from here that their galleys sailed out to hold the kyles in fee, for 'Saucy Mary' of Castle Maol was not the only one who could claim a toll. But later the Mackinnons decided in favour of a more modern house and built Strathaird, still to be seen up a short drive to the right of the road. The family were staunch Jacobites and the delightful pledge 'To the little gentleman in black velvet' may often have been drunk beneath its hospitable roof.

As is well known, Prince Charles, after his night at Kingsburgh, left Skye for Raasay, but he shortly returned again, Raasay having proved even more dangerous. This time he came disguised as the servant of Malcolm Macleod, Macleod of Raasay's younger brother. Macleod bethought him of Mackinnon, but by now the hunt was drawing in and to take the Prince to the house of a known Jacobite was deemed unsafe. So Macleod guided him through the

Cuchullins into Strathaird and hid him in the house of his brother-in-law, John Mackinnon. On their arrival their unsuspecting host was from home, and Malcolm, 'trusting no woman's tongue', said no more to his sister than that his servant was exhausted and in need of rest and shelter. Then, leaving the Prince with her, he went in search of his brother-in-law. What was their horror to find on their return that the Prince, like his celebrated forebear, was 'minding' the scones and also the baby.

Mackinnon, on being made aware of this illustrious arrival, hastened to wait on the Prince and to conceal him in 'Prince Charlie's Cave', on the shore of Loch Scavaig beyond Elgol. There Lady Mackinnon furnished him with a bed and food. The story goes that one of her maids came upon her carrying a newly roasted duck and a covered dish. The girl, curious, offered to carry them for her. 'No, no', said Lady Mackinnon, with more presence of mind than truth, 'I am taking them to a wounded fox I found. It knows me now but you might fright it. Do not speak of this for if your master hears he will kill the poor creature.' The maid commented later: 'Then I knew it was the Prince, for it was herself that was forever angry at the foxes.' Actually, several trusted members of the household were in the secret. Mackinnon arranged for a boat and chose two young Mackinnons to row the Prince to Mallaig. They successfully made their way there on the night of 4 July, only hidden from the warships which were searching the kyle for them by the fierceness of a storm of wind and rain. So ended the Prince's sojourn in Skye and so, shortly afterwards, began a year's imprisonment for the old chief.

To the left of the road is a small bay where the river Abhain Cill Mhaire goes out to sea. A side-road runs along the river bank, passing Kilmarie Lodge, to the old graveyard of Kilmarie, strange, unexpected, and rather desolate, with the pebbles of the seashore reaching to its gates. It has been planted with yew and cypress; purple flags and red-hot pokers bloom among the graves, giving it a charm unique among Skye burial-grounds, most of which are neglected, dreary, and repellent.

The site of the old church of Kilmarie and of the stone circle whose proximity no doubt originally called it into being are now no longer to be seen. The ruins of the old church, I am told, were swept away by the sea during that great storm in the 1920's which also blew down the Dunvegan woods. The storm followed not long after the burial near the old church of an unknown sailor taken from the sea, and there were those who believed this to be the cause of the church's disappearance, for, as the old Gaelic rhyme says: 'the sea will search the four russet divisions of the universe to find her children', and Kenneth Macleod advises that a body taken from the sea should always be buried near the water's edge, or the sea, desiring to recover her own, will flood much land in search of it.

This church is said to have stood on the site of an older church of St. Maelrhuba (Servant of Peace) who was the patron saint of south-eastern Skye. He had a chapel at Kilmolruy in Bracadale, also one on Loch Eynort, and all Bracadale kept a 'tryst' on his day. But Strath was the real scene of his labours.

St. Maelrhuba was a follower of St. Columba's teaching and was Abbot of Bangor in Ireland. In about 673 to 676 he felt a call to follow in St. Columba's footsteps and so came to Scotland as a missionary to the northern Scots and Picts, and in due course he reached Skye. It was to Broadford Bay that he is supposed to have come in his coracle from the great monastery at Applecross. With him he brought his bell and hung it upon a tree. Here it was dumb all the week, no matter what winds blew, but every Sunday its voice was heard pealing through the hills. It is recorded that after the death of the saint his bell was brought into the church for safe keeping, whereupon it became 'dumb' for ever and the tree upon which it used to hang withered and died.

In the early Celtic Church every abbot had his handbell with which to summon his monks to prayer or work: this was his badge of office and sometimes his only personal possession. These bells were therefore much sought after as relics. They themselves closely resembled the modern cowbell, being of the simplest possible construction, but after a saint's death his bell would be preserved either by his family or his church, and in later centuries many were enclosed in jewelled reliquaries of gold or silver, highly wrought. But always after a saint's death his bell became 'dumb', none but he having the right to use it. This may be the origin of the story.

Near here was the cell of that Mackinnon who later became one of the abbots of Iona. Between Kilmarie and Strathaird House lie the ruins of yet another church, Kirkabost, Church of the Homestead. This is said to have been built by a Norseman, once owner of what would now be the Home Farm, on being converted to Christianity in about the year 1000. Near it are Na Clachan Breitheach, the Lying, or False, Stones, a name presumably given to them by Christian converts. These were once, if tradition is to be believed, Stones of Wisdom who could both foretell the future and show justice as between man and man.

After Kilmarie the road runs down the centre of the peninsula for some miles, finally crossing to the shores of Loch Scavaig, where it ends at the township of Elgol. To the left of the road along the shore of Loch Slapin lie many duns and at least one prehistoric tomb: this part must once have been very strongly fortified. It is in the cliffs of this coast, on the Point of Eels on the farm of Glashnakill, that the once famous Spar Cave is to be found. A boat is necessary to reach it. This was one of the sights of Skye in the time of Sir Walter Scott and is believed to have contained as fine a display of stalactites as any to be seen in the Cheddar Caves today. Scott wrote of it:

> *And o'er his head the dazzling Spars*
> *Gleam like a firmament of stars.*

Unfortunately the cave was despoiled. Many of its loveliest spars were carried away as souvenirs, a fashion which is obviously neither new nor American. Others were ground down to provide lime for the fields, so that now much of its beauty is a thing of the past.

In Gaelic it was called Sloched Altrimen, Cave of the Nursling, because once, when the 'Princes of Skye' were away fighting the Picts under Anlaive, King of Norway, MacCairbe, King of Ulster, attacked the Hebrides and carried off Colonsay's son as hostage. The 'Lords of Skye' on their return immediately invaded Ulster, not only rescuing the hostage but carrying off the Ulster King's daughter as well. On the homeward voyage, however, their fleet was entirely destroyed by storm, one ship reaching Loch Slapin and being wrecked there. A Skye princess, Dounhuila, was watching the storm from her father's stronghold, Dunglas. Seeing the ship in danger she bade her men rescue the crew, and among those saved was young 'Colonsay' and his dog, but as her father and his were at enmity he was held prisoner in the dun. The young people speedily fell in love and ultimately a son was born to

Dounhuila. In fear of death should her father discover the boy, she hid him, in the care of her old nurse, in the Spar Cave. Colonsay's dog was their guard from wild beasts, and legends of a haunted cave where mermaids sang and drove all men mad kept them free from discovery. Meanwhile Dounhuila helped her lover to escape. He returned at once to Colonsay and succeeded in making peace between the two families, and then suggested that the peace might be ratified by a marriage between himself and Dounhuila. This also was agreed to. Perhaps her parents were not as blind as she appears to have believed: however that may be, after the wedding she and 'Colonsay', nurse, nursling, and dog returned in peace to Colonsay.

Overlooking Elgol is Bidein an Fhithich. Near here once stood the famous Raven's Stone, about which the Brahn Seer prophesied. It is believed that this prophecy, however, can never be fulfilled, as seventy or eighty years ago the stone was broken up and the main portion of it is now incorporated in one wall of the Glendale church, according to the Rev. A. R. Forbes's *Place Names of Skye*. The stone was believed to have had some connexion with old pagan religious ceremonies.

Elgol itself is said to have acquired its name as follows. There is a tradition that Vortigern once sent Aella with five ships to 'explore' the Western Isles, but the inhabitants of Skye did not like being explored, so Picts and Scots, joining together, raised what ships they could and intercepted him at the mouth of Loch Scavaig, where a great battle was fought. Vortigern's ships were driven off but Aella's name remained to be enshrined in the first syllable of Elgol.

Beyond Elgol, on the eoast, lies Prince Charlie's Cave, before referred to. Some claim this to be the cave in which one of the earlier Mackinnon chiefs, being attacked by a wolf, slew the creature by forcing a deer bone down its throat, a feat still commemorated in the Mackinnon arms.

It is said that in the early days one Maclier held part of Strath and incurred the anger of Olave, King of Man and the Isles; how, we do not know, but he must have been a man of some power and importance, for the King brought to visit him a sizable fleet and Maclier was put to death. But the expedition was not an entirely happy one for Olave either, if legend is to be believed, for among his ships were those of Somerled, the first Macdonald to appear in Skye history. In those days the Macdonalds, though already a power on the mainland, had not seized Sleat and so had no foothold in Skye. Somerled desired to marry Raynhild, Olave's daughter, but her father had other views. A friend of Somerled's called 'Maurice' undertook to overcome Olave's resistance to the marriage and obtain Raynhild's hand for his chief. This he did in this wise. He claimed for his master's galley the right to sail next the King's. Then, in the night, when the ships were beached, he made many holes in the King's ship and filled them with tallow. In due course, off Ardnamurchan Point, the tallow began to melt and Olave's ship to fill and sink. Thereupon Somerled's galley approached and offered the King safety in return for the hand of his daughter. Olave accepted but never forgave.

Roads are few and far between in Strath. Besides the road to Elgol there is one other, connecting Harrapool, on the main Kyleakin–Broadford road, with the township of Heast on Loch-an-Eilean, a part of Loch Eisort. About two miles beyond Heast was the stone circle of Boreraig, as usual well defended by duns and, again as usual, close by the circle is the ruin of a little Celtic church, Teampuill Chaon, Chapel of Congan or Comgal. Near Boreraig, too, was the Knee Stone. This was a stone, eight feet long and two feet six inches wide, which some men wished to use as a bridge across a small burn, but, having built supports for it, they could not lift the stone on to them. Mackinnon, who was passing by, inquired what the trouble was and, on being told, lifted the stone single-handed, 'though with an effort', into position and then supported one end on his knee while masons fixed the other. It is not surprising that the early Mackinnons had a great reputation for strength. Indeed, it has been suggested that this clan descended on the distaff side from the Fienne giants.

It is said to have been in Loch Eisort that three small children went to sleep in a boat, and woke to find the wind and tide had risen and the boat had broken loose. Terrified, the mites, without sail or oars (and too young to use them if there had been any), drifted out towards the dreaded kyles. From shouting, they fell to quiet, exhausted weeping, for it seemed no one heard. But the Birds of Bride had heard and had seen: like gleaming white crosses, they flew as fast as wings could carry them to the little chapel of Kilbride on the hill overlooking the loch in search of their mistress, St. Bride, and soon the tired children saw a lovely lady, her arms full of bog-cotton, walking across the sea. She dropped the soft cotton heads into the boat and bade the babies curl up on it and sleep, for now they were safe. And so only a lone fisherman saw the blaze of love and glory which brought the boat ashore.

Peace be to thee and thy children, O Skye,
Dearest of islands.

(ALEXANDER NICOLSON)

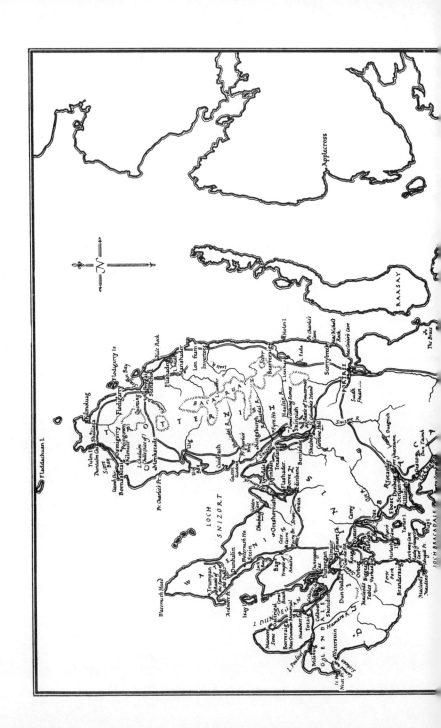

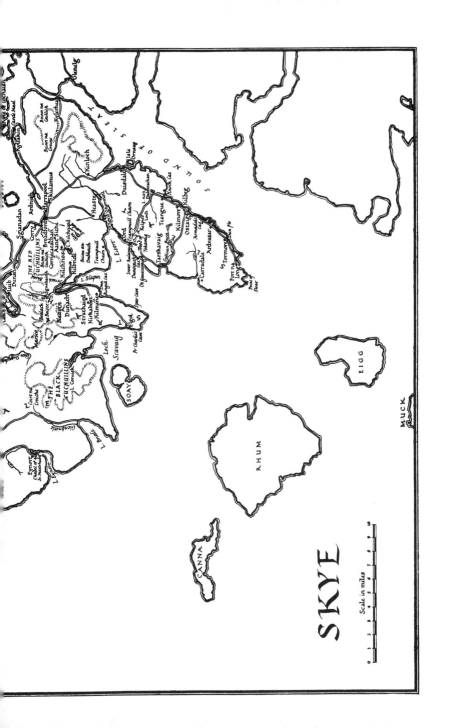

SKYE

Scale in miles

Index